# WOMEN OF THE REFORMATION

## From Spain to Scandinavia

# WOMEN OF THE REFORMATION

## From Spain to Scandinavia

**ROLAND H. BAINTON**

AUGSBURG PUBLISHING HOUSE
MINNEAPOLIS, MINNESOTA

WOMEN OF THE REFORMATION, From Spain to Scandinavia

Copyright © 1977 Augsburg Publishing House

Library of Congress Catalog Card No. 76-27089

International Standard Book No. 0-8066-1568-0

Scripture quotations unless otherwise noted are from the Revised Standard Version of the Bible, copyright 1946, 1952, and 1971 by the Division of Christian Education of the National Council of Churches.

*Strand 9.95/5.00*
*4/26/78*

MANUFACTURED IN THE UNITED STATES OF AMERICA

# Contents

*To*
*my great granddaughters*
*Rachel*
*Sylvia*
*Libbey Catherine*

# Acknowledgements

This volume has been more of a cooperative task than any of the preceding because so many countries are covered, involving languages in their sixteenth century forms. I am very grateful to colleagues at Yale and the community of scholars for assistance. On the Spanish material I owe a debt to José Nieto, Angela Selke Barbudo, Antonio Marquez and Tessa Ortega Emmart. For Denmark I have had help from Harald Ingholt of Yale and Leif Crane of Copenhagen. Sixteenth century Norwegian would have left me unsteady save for Nils and Birgitte Dahl of Yale and Sigrid Osberg of Bergen. For Sweden I would have been at a loss for a copy of her correspondence in seven languages had one not been supplied by the Brigham Young University library at Provo, Utah. Polish studies owe much to contacts made for me by Carol Borowski and meetings with Lech Szczucki and Waclaw Urban. On the Hungarian material I am indebted to Stephen Benko, Imre Mihaly, Eva Balogh of Yale and in Rumania, Nagy Geza and László Makkal. The task of rendering sixteenth century German into twentieth century English verse profited from suggestions by Barbara Green. Mrs. Price checked the manuscript. Suzanne Selinger has identified bibliographical references and the help of Andrea Foster for interlibrary loans has been invaluable. I am indebted to Marjorie Wynne for help and permissions in the Beinecke Library of Yale University.

I have permission from the Student Christian Movement Press of London to reprint with some changes the article which appeared with the title "Feminine Piety in Tudor England" in the volume *Christian Spirituality; Essays in honour of Gordon Rupp,* edited by Peter Brooks.

Similarly I am permitted to reprint with alterations the article "Queen Katarina Jagellonica," which appeared in *Theological Soundings,* Notre Dame Seminary Jubilee Studies, 1923-73. Permission is granted by this seminary in New Orleans.

# Preface

A few reflections are in order at the close of these three volumes. Why was the study undertaken? Because of a lifelong interest in those who have not had their due. In 1955 the Dudleian lecture at Harvard was on *The Office of the Minister's Wife in New England*. The larger study followed the death of Ruth Woodruff Bainton in the hope of rendering a posthumous tribute to one widely loved but little acclaimed.

A further purpose is to correct historical distortions. Women were not enslaved throughout the past, as some seem to think. To be sure, they had a rough time by reason of circumstances which affected all. In the sixteenth century the average length of life was around twenty five years, because of high infant mortality. To replenish the population after devastating plagues families of ten or so were required. Women in consequence spent one segment of their lives mothering and another grandmothering. They had to be supported by men and were glad to be. And think not that the lot of men was easy with families of a wife and some ten children to support.

Certainly in our day we should assist women to enter into all of those fields which our new circumstances make possible. To that end history is not to be distorted. But is a male in a position to correct it? Is he capable of telling how women felt in the sixteenth century? Perhaps not. But he can record how they said they felt, provided they said anything at all. And there is the rub.

They may have kept their resentments to themselves so that their real feelings can only be divined. But let not a modern woman think she can divine them by projecting herself into a bygone culture. Take the case of Katherine Zell, who, having lost two children in infancy and incapable of more, believed herself to be suffering from God's displeasure. A modern woman would go straight to the doctor to learn what was amiss and whether there could be a correction. One must spend years with the literature of an earlier time to have a feeling for its ethos.

As for the role of women covered in these volumes, one observes that administrative functions in the church were exercised only by queens who, by virtue of their office, could not avoid involvement. They had either to manipulate the political structure or accommodate. Catherine de Medici, to avert civil war, convened the Colloquy of Poissy and having failed, instigated the massacre of Saint Bartholomew. Elizabeth I endeavored to "comprehend" all England in a common church by allowing wide latitude in dogma along with conformity in externals. The Puritans disrupted her scheme and the end was toleration of minorities. Isabella of Spain sought to unify Spanish culture in terms of rigid Catholicism. Bona Sforza in Poland accepted religious pluralism because it already existed. Katherine of Sweden, to bring her country back to Rome, made accommodations to Lutherans which Rome would not tolerate. Isabella of Transylvania proclaimed full religious liberty primarily because the Turkish overlord so required.

A pastoral ministry to the ailing and indigent was open to women in every age of the church. A sacramental ministry, save for emergency baptism, was denied alike by Catholics and mainline Protestants, except in the case of abbesses, who during the Middle Ages, filled fully the role of bishops.[1] The preaching ministry was allowed only by radical sects, having often a preponderance of women.[2] During the Reformation one turns to the Alumbrados and Antitrinitarians and in the seventeenth century to the Quakers.

This phenomenon may be explained partly on sociological grounds because in the sects the women found greater scope, but there is also a strong religious factor. The sects in question placed more stress on piety than on dogma and this stance was congenial to women, whether within or without the established church structures. Women wrote devotional literature rather than systematic theology. We recall the *Rime Religiose* of Vittoria Colonna, the *Chansons Spirituelles* of Marguerite of Navarre, the meditations of Katherine Zell, the *Lamentations of a Sinful Soul of Katherine Parr.* We shall encounter the *Modliwity* (prayers) of Polish women. I am puzzled to account for this phenomenon. Have women refrained from theology because they were not supposed to exceed their sphere or because they were not interested?

These volumes have not been written by reason of an exclusive concern for women, but also to discover how, regardless of sex, people felt in every aspect of life. Why the readiness "to let goods and kindred go, this mortal life also"? The core of piety is to be found not simply through creeds and confessions but in the contexts of living, dying, uniting, dividing, loving, hating, understanding and misunderstanding. One must not neglect *Institutes of the Christian Religion* and *Loci Communes,* but the core of piety is better found in letters charged with passion, written in tears or chanted in ecstasies. The anguish and the joy are often most intense in the words exchanged between husband and wife, children and parents.

The biographical approach throws light also on social changes. Did religion play a role in the breakdown of the system of family-made marriages in the western world? There were undoubtedly many factors. One was the romanticizing of marriage. Courtly love was at first extra-matrimonial, though not promiscuous. Prior to the Reformation it was beginning to be conjoined with marriage. And romantic love is obviously an individual affair. The Reformation broke with the authority of the church and at times with the authority of parents. Unity of faith was deemed needful for a successful marriage and since faith was individualized, marriage was personalized. Is there any evidence in these volumes that such was the case? There is some, but an extensive verification of the hypothesis calls for a study of the following century.

Of incidental personal interest to me has been the heightened awareness of the interrelations of European society. I knew already the contacts of the English printers with Basel, the residence of the Marian exiles on the continent and of the English Recusants in Spain, of the Italians in Geneva and Poland, of the Poles in all of the universities of Europe and of the half dozen nationalities in the Church of the Strangers at London. But I was startled to find that the Italian queen of Poland needed a safe conduct from the queen of England in order to return to her own country. The real point was permission from Philip of Spain and lord also of Naples. He was married to the English queen. Hence the safe conduct was from Philip and Mary. I was surprised to discover that the king of Sweden was bargaining to sell a fleet either to Spain to crush the Netherlands or to the Netherlands to throw off Spain. I had not looked to find Sir Philip Sidney in Cracow, let alone to read a letter from the king of Poland to the Sultan beginning "dearest brother." I had not expected to find Lady Russell clandestinely disemminating in England the views of Caspar Schwenckfeld. And I was bowled over to be shown the title page of a Spanish devotional tract in Mexico with a woodcut adapted from the first edition of the English Book of Common Prayer.

Perhaps the most revealing discovery is that no one of these sketches is a success story. Prophets always die disappointed because achievements never equal aspirations. These women walked as seeing Him that is invisible sustained by faith that somehow their toils and troubles had a place in the grand design.

## NOTES

1. Morris, Joan, *The Lady Was a Bishop* (New York, 1973).
2. Lerner, Robert E., *The Heresy of the Free Spirit in the Later Middle Ages* (University of California, Berkeley, 1972), p. 230, note 5.

# SPAIN

Spain long before the sixteenth century had been confronted with the choice of alignment either with Christendom beyond the Pyranees or with Islam beyond the straits. For some time the peninsula had harbored three religions: Christianity, Judaism and Islam. The three had achieved a measure of accommodation and cultural interchange. Wars were sometimes not confessional. Christians and Moors fought Moors and Christians. But as the fifteenth century advanced, the fever of national consolidation apparent in France and England affected Spain also. And the Catholic kings resolved to achieve both political and cultural unification in terms of Catholic orthodoxy. Ferdinand and Isabella were the main driving forces, he from the political, she from the religious angle. The Inquisition was introduced in 1478 and Torquemada made Grand Inquisitor in 1483. In 1492 the Jews were given the choice of exile or baptism. Many left, many were baptized. These latter were called *Marranos*. In the same years Granada fell. Later on the Moors were given the same choice as the Jews. Converted Muslims were called *Moriscos*. Both were characterized as *conversos*. To keep them from lapsing into the practices of their ancestral religions the Inquisition became more rigorous.

A measure of relaxation occurred in the early decades of the sixteenth century as the humanism of the Renaissance invaded the peninsula. Cardinal Ximenes, the primate of Spain and for a

# COPILACION

delas Inftructiones del Officio dela fancta Inquifici
on hechas por el muy Reuerendo feñor fray Tho
mas de Torquemada Prior del monafterio de fanctà
cruz de Segouia primero Inquifidor general delos
reynos y feñorios de Efpaña : E por los otros Reue
rendiffimos feñores Inquifidores genarales q defpues
fuccedieron cerca dela orden que fe ha de tener enel
exercicio del fancto officio donde van pueftas fucceff
uaméte por fu parte todas las inftructiontes q tocan a
los Inquifidores E a otra parte las q tocā a cada vno
delos officiales y miniftros del fancto Officio las qua
les fe copilárō enla manera q dicha es por mādado del
Illuftriffimo y Reuerédiffimo feñor dõ Alōfo manrri
que Cardenal delos doze apoftoles Arcobifpo de Se
uilla Inquifidor general de Efpaña.

Compilation of the Instructions for the Office of the Holy Inquisition
made by the Very Reverend Friar Thomas of Torquemada.

time the regent, though medieval enough in his asceticism and crusading fervor, favored the new learning, founded the university of Alcala and projected the Complutensian Polyglot, which for the first time printed the entire Bible in the original tongues. In such an atmosphere the great Christian humanist, Erasmus, enjoyed a great popularity.

But such latitude did not outlast the 1520s. Erasmus, while still esteemed by the humanists, was attacked by the Spanish monks. The "errors" of the Alumbrados were condemned in 1525. The emergence of Luther caused Spain to panic at the prospect of the disintegration of that very Christendom with which she had sought to be aligned. The Inquisition was the more invoked. At the time of the great *auto da fé* of the Lutherans in 1559, Cardinal Carranza, lately returned from assisting Mary Tudor to eradicate Protestantism by burnings, was himself incarcerated by the Inquisition for seventeen years until his vindication in time to say Mass once and die. The degree of the hysteria is evident in that one of the charges levelled against him was that on hearing of someone praying the "Our Father" to Saint Peter, he had said "Of course it's not right, but it won't do any harm." [1] There were, naturally, more serious counts but that such a peccadillo should have been deemed worthy of mention indicates the extent of the paranoia.

Three groups came under attack: the Alumbrados or Illuminists, the Erasmians and the Lutherans. The differences between these three are not to be overdone. The Alumbrados had in common with the Erasmians the view that the rites of the church are valueless as external performances. They agreed with the Lutherans on the worthlessness of good works for the attainment of salvation and on the denial of purgatory and indulgences. The big difference was the focusing of their piety on God the Father and the Spirit rather than God the Son. The Lutherans, in turn, were not as remote as is often assumed from the Erasmians. The main point of difference was that Erasmus was still in the church whereas Luther had been cast out.

The Alumbrados were groups with little formal organization, who met in conventicles under inspired leaders. Their total numbers were considerable. The constituency drew heavily from three sources: conversos, Franciscans and women.

The conversos from Judaism were attracted by a type of Christianity which did not center on Christ, though his words could be used to justify reliance on the spirit, for did he not say, "It is the spirit that gives life. the flesh is of no avail"? They could see in his sufferings a foretaste of their own, but hesitated to call him God save in the sense that there is "that of God" in all.

The oppressed find solace either by way of time or of the timeless. The device of time is to posit surcease in a future age, in a restoration of paradise, when the spirit of the Lord will cover the earth as the waters cover the sea. Spain in this period had many apocalyptic movements, but we find no such dreams among the Alumbrados. They were disposed rather to take refuge in the timelessness of God's invading love, to be filled with the spirit of the Ancient of Days, in whom there is no shadow of turning, no yesterday, today or tomorrow. Mysticism may take the form of the loss of the self in the great abyss of being or in milder fashion of the divine indwelling, the inflooding of the spirit as the light that lights every man coming into the world. With all of these types Christ may be a prototype, an example, but scarcely the second person of the Trinity, consubstantial with the Father. This is not to say that the Alumbrados made any such specific denials. The stress was elsewhere.

The Franciscans had in their heritage many elements which would make them hospitable to the concepts of the Alumbrados. The emphasis was on the spirit. The rule of St. Francis was given by the *Spirito Santo* and had, therefore, greater authority than the dictates of the church. The Franciscans, who disobeyed the church, were in trouble and the radical branch of the Fraticelli was suppressed. Some of the Franciscans so relied on the spirit as to consider scholarship needless for the interpretation of Scripture. There were, to be sure, Franciscan scholars, but the Capuchins, originating in this very period in Italy as a branch of the Franciscan family, decried learning in their early period. Similarly among the Alumbrados we find the untutored, including women, claiming to be better able to expound the Bible through the spirit than were the learned without it. One is tempted to think of the Alumbrados as heirs of the Franciscan Spirituals and the Fraticelli, but there was this difference that the Franciscans were very Christ centered. Finally the Alumbrados attracted women. We have just commented on the great penchant of women for mystical movements and radical sects. We shall find examples as we examine the inquisitorial trials.

## BIBLIOGRAPHY

### BACKGROUND FOR SPAIN IN THE FIFTEENTH CENTURY

Longhurst, John, *The Age of Torquemada* (Lawrence, Kansas, 1964).
Bainton, Roland H., *El Alma Hispana y el Alma Sajona* (Buenos Aires, 1961)
Oro, Jose Garcia, *Cisneros y la Reforma del Clero Español en Tiempo de los Reyes Catolicos* (Madrid, 1971).
FOR THE MEDIEVAL SECTS.
Koch, Gottfried, "Frauenfrage und Ketzertum im Mittelalter," *Forschungen zu Mittelalterlichen Geschichte* IX (Berlin, 1962).
Lerner, Robert, *The Heresy of the Free Spirit* (University of California Press, 1922). On the role of women p. 230 note 5.

### RELIGIOUS MOVEMENTS IN SPAIN IN THE EARLY SIXTEENTH CENTURY

Longhurst, John, *Luther's Ghost in Spain* (Lawrence, Kansas, 1969). Examples of Alumbrados, Erasmians and Lutherans both men and women, with a good bibliography.
Bataillon, Marcel, *Erasmo y España* (Mexico City, 1966), much enlarged over the earlier French edition.
Marquez, Antonio, *Los Alumbrados* (Taurus ed., Madrid, 1972).
Llorca, Bernardino, *Die Spanische Inquisition und die Alumbrados* (Berlin, 1933).
Nieto, Jose, *Juan Valdes* (Geneva, 1970), analizes Alcaraz.
Priem, Hans Jürger, *Francisca Ossuna*, 2 vols. (Hamburg, 1967).
Ros, Fidele de, *Le Père François d'Osuna* (Paris, 1937).

## NOTE

1. Idigoras, José Ignacio Tellechea, *El Arzobispo Carranza y su Tiempo* (Madrid, 1968) I, p. 155.

# Isabel de la Cruz

We now turn to the records of the trials. Isabel de la Cruz, the reputed founder of the Alumbrados, was of the stock of the conversos. She left home against the wish of her mother because the family was worldly and Christ said, "He that loves father and mother more than me is not worthy of me." [1] Isabel is not for that reason to be regarded as a congenital rebel, seeing that disobedience to parents for the sake of religion was the one form of defiance acceptable in that age. She became a Franciscan tertiary with the title of *beata*.

In 1512 she began to disseminate her views of religion at Guadalajara and soon had a considerable following among the Franciscans and in the higher echelons of the church. She was arrested by the Inquisition in 1524 largely because of the delation of a one-time disciple, Mari Nuñex. Isabel was incarcerated under frequent interrogation over a span of five years until her condemnation in 1529.

Our knowledge of her views is derived chiefly from the confession made after years of intimidation and torture. The admissions may not have been altogether accurate, since elicited under such pressures. The text of the confession comes to us only because incorporated in the record of the trial of her disciple Alcaraz, also of the conversos. Since he named her as his source we may regard his tenets as a systematic formulation of her own. The record of his trial includes also the sentence pro-

18

nounced against him. In addition we have an edict of 1525 against the errors of the Alumbrados, not all of which are necessarily to be ascribed to Isabel and Alcaraz.

But there is no need for reservation as to the core of their theology. The foci were two: the love of God and the interiorizing of religion. God, as love, invades man and is more truly present in man than in the sacrament.[2] Man, thus infused, loves God in return and likewise the neighbor. God, being love, does not condemn any one to eternal torment. Hell is concocted to frighten, as when one says to a child, "The bogey man'll get

Methods of torture in the sixteenth century.

you if you don't be good." [3] There is no hell. The church, which is the spouse of the God of mercy, ought not to consign to hell by excommunications.[4] At the very mention of such Isabel would wave her arms in derision. She did not, however, object to purgatory, for it is not inconsistent with the love of God to allow a period of purgation in preparation for heaven.[5]

Man's response to the love of God should be an absolute surrender of the human will to the divine will. "Except the seed falls into the ground and dies it bears no fruit. He who loves his life loses it." [6] So he who works to save his soul loses it and he who loses his soul in God saves it.[7] Evangelical perfection consists in the negation of one's own will. This renunciation is called in Spanish *dexamiento* [8] (the German equivalent is *Gelassenheit*). The surrender to God may involve resistance to men. Disobedience to parents and superiors is mandatory if they go counter to the love of God.[9]

The surrender of one's own will excludes any attempt to manipulate God for one's own ends. Seek not to scale heaven or evade hell.[10] Take no thought as to election. Leave all to God according to his good pleasure. Prayer is not to be petition for any one thing in particular. Lay before God the heart's desires, adding, "Thy will be done." [11] Consequently good works done for the sake of credit are reprehensible and the attempt to reduce penalties for sins by bulls of indulgence is abhorrent.[12]

Being in the love of God has certain consequences. Man will not necessarily be perfect. A lapse is possible, but it will be minor and pardonable.[13] The corollary is that, as man can be united with God, so also with the devil. He had thrown Isabel into a perfect hell by tempting her to take her life. Collapsing after the long ordeal, she gave the explanation that as a benighted woman she had been seduced by the Evil One.[14]

The second great focus was the interiorizing of religion. This was in part a deduction from the presence of God in the soul rather than in the body. Here entered a strain of the Neoplatonic dualism of flesh and spirit, that is of the corporeal and the incorporeal. The body is a weight upon the spirit. Did not Jesus say, "The spirit gives life. The flesh is of no avail"? [15] The result of this dichotomy is a disparagement of all the sensory expressions of religion, whether of music through the ear, pictures through the eye, the sacrament through the mouth, or liturgical gestures through the body.

Music for Isabel received no recorded attention. Images were disparaged, save for the cross and the crucifix, and even here it were better to bear the cross in one's heart. What a paltry view of God has he who needs an image to bring him to mind! [16] As for Our Lady, any living woman is a better image than a dead statue.[17] Bodily postures are without avail: genuflections, bowing at the name of Jesus, kissing the ground when the priest says *Et homo factus est* (And was made man); standing for the Gospel, folding the hands in prayer and sprinkling with holy water.

One would suppose that castigations of the body would be recommended to keep down the lusts of the flesh. On the contrary, flagellation, hair shirts and fasting were highly disapproved. They were in part disparaged as good works designed to win divine favor, but partly, one suspects, as physical devices for overcoming the physical. At the same time the physical was given its own sphere along side of which the spirit could still be operative. In conjugal union God could be as much present as in prayer.[18] Pilgrimages and holy days were discountenanced because the spirit is not limited either to place or time.[19]

With respect to modes of prayer, the surrender of the self applied not only to the will but also to the mind. One should not be impeded by liturgical forms recited by rote and out loud. Rather one should meditate without concentration on some particular theme. Leave the mind entirely free for the invasion of the spirit. This was called mental prayer, as opposed to vocal prayer, stigmatized as nothing but "breath." [20] During the Mass, Isabel was revolted by the practice of worshipers saying interminable *Ave Marias,* as if there were value in the count. Isn't one enough? We are not saved by *calculus.*[21] For herself, she would rather stand during the Eucharist in awed silence before the mystery of redemption.[22]

Although she was quite capable of affronting popular feeling by going counter to current practices, at times she would conform to avoid offense. Although in church she disliked the liturgical forms, she had been seen at night in her room reading the hours by candle light.[23] There is no evidence that she kept any image but she did recognize that images are the text books of the unlearned.[24] The point was not that these outward practices were inherently wrong, but simply unnecessary, indifferent and often distracting.

Reliance on the spirit raised a question with respect to authority in religion. Isabel recognized the authority of the Bible, but how is it to be interpreted? The answer was that if one dwelt in the love of God, one would be kept free from error.[25] This is why she, an untutored woman, had the audacity to set herself above the doctors in expounding the Word of God.[26] Did not Paul say, "The letter kills. The spirit gives life."?[27] At the same time the spirit does not unravel all mysteries, since there is that which "hath not entered the heart of man." One should not indulge in vain curiosity.[28] We thus find a vein of anti-intellectualism in the spiritualizing of religion.

The thought of Isabel was systematized by her disciple Alcaraz, who claimed to have received all of his ideas from her. Actually not quite all. Unlike her he recognized the principle of obedience to the church and did not claim, as she had done, inerrancy for himself as an exegete of Scripture.[29] He was entirely at one with her, however, as to the externals of worship and was claimed to have affronted public feeling by attending Mass in unseemly garb and with a large hat, in order, he said, to cover a gash on his scalp.[30]

On several counts he was more explicit than his teacher. One was the rejection of music as an aid to religion. A friend said to him that the sweet chants and hymns of the church were ordained by the Holy Spirit to make glad the heart of man. Alcaraz rejected them as external.[31] Another point was the superiority of *dexamiento* to *recogimiento*. The first, as we have noted, was simply leaving the mind open for the spirit to blow "as it listeth." *Recogimiento* was not recollection in the sense of remembering but re-collection, pulling oneself together, concentrating on some special theme as in the *Spiritual Exercises* of Loyola. For Alcaraz such a scheme was too rigid.[32]

The most significant elaboration of her thought had to do with the mystical doctrine of the indwelling of God in man. Alcaraz was familiar among others with Climacus, Bernard, Bonaventura, Gerson and Dionysius the Areopagite.[33] They were mystics not in the sense of experiencing raptures so much as in sensing the union of God with man, though, of course, there might be ecstatic transports. Alcaraz is credited with saying that the love of God in man is God himself in man.[34] This was a slight rephrasing of 1 John 4:16, "God is love, and he who abides in love abides in God, and God abides in him."

This presence of God in man is what the Quakers call "that of God in every man." The medieval mystics spoke of the spark or the seed in the soul. These can be cultivated and increased. The spark may be fanned, the seed sprinkled. Dionysius posited three stages which Alcaraz elaborated as: 1) purification through contrition; 2) illumination through contemplation of God's gifts in creation and redemption. Here he allowed meditation on the passion of Christ, which Isabel rejected; 3) union of the soul with God, the most perfect of the three.[35]

Here is an example of what this doctrine meant to him in his own experience. He wrote:

> It is of God that there is in me no honor or preferment that any should envy, save that *God dwells in my heart and works* (Italics mine). These are my riches. Though I be but a foul sinner, I question not the goodness of God. I am blessed with the knowledge of the truth and the love of it. In the writings of the saints I have abundant examples and this is why I steep myself in holy exercises to free myself from many ills, to give me good desires and to withdraw me from evil doers. Although it is I that say this, I do so because God has done it, that I may give the glory unto him from whom proceeds every good coming down from the Father of Lights.[36]

Some interpreters see in Isabel and Alcaraz anticipations of Luther. To be sure Isabel, like Luther, rejected indulgences, but the reasons were different. Luther's point was that there is absolutely no treasury of the saints transferable by the pope to those in arrears. Isabel stressed rather that, even if there were, to seek from it a benefit for oneself would be abhorrent. There is a measure of similarity between the Alumbrados and the early

*Isabel de la Cruz*

## THE CELESTIAL LADDER
## OF CLIMACUS

Climacus was one of the sources of the ideas of Alcaraz and presumably of Isabel. The name Climacus was the sobriquet of John, the abbot of Mount Sinai at the close of the sixth century. The word "climacus" is from the Greek meaning ladder, from which also our word climax is derived. John's work entitled *The Celestial Ladder,* had a great vogue and was speedily translated from the Greek into Latin and the vernaculars, including Spanish. It was also frequently illustrated. The accompanying example has been redrawn for clarity from a faint reproduction of a twelfth century manuscript. The rungs are numbered from bottom up in Greek notation. Within the rungs were the titles of the chapters, in this instance, nearly illegible and therefore omitted in the drawing. The artist has added a few features not in the text. At the top is Christ holding two crowns, at the bottom a dragon signifying hell. Such a borrowing from the Last Judgment is not consonant with Climacus' pre-occupation with the love of God and one may assume that he would not have been happy over the portrayal of the poor fellow, who had made the last rung, only then to be so carried away by overweening, self-confidence as to be sent careening down to the dragon's jaws. Isabel and Alcaraz would have relished the twenty-eighth rung where private prayer is said to be in no need of bodily postures. The final rung expresses the core of the piety of the Alumbrados, for "when we are boiling with the love of God, when we are united and kneaded into the divine love, the body itself exhibits, as it were in a mirror, serenity and splendor, just as when Moses came down from the mount, his face shone."

Luther under the influence of the mystics Tauler and the *Theologia Germanica,* but the later Luther rejected all mysticism and so separated man from God that man's only hope of peace with God lies not in an infusion of being but in an act of sheer grace.

The spiritualizing of religion was also alien to Luther. The dichotomy of God and man did not carry over into the relation of spirit and body. Therefore in worship he responded to pictures, liturgy and music. Especially when it came to Scripture he would not lay claim to the key of David to unlock the Word through the spirit, regardless of scholarship. Above all, Luther was aghast at such individualizing of religion that corporate forms dissolve into vague fellowships. His word for the spiritualists was *Schwärmer,* fanatics. He had in mind the ilk of Denck, Franck, Münster and Schwenckfeld, whom he called *Stenckfeld* (Stinkfield).

What now in the views of Isabel and Alcaraz offended the Inquisition? Not the mild mysticism of Climacus, Dionysius, Bernard, Bonaventura and Gerson, although the church is always leery of mysticism because it tends to undercut history. Christianity is a historical religion, arising from an event in time when the Word became flesh. This is a historical event which the mystics tended to transform into a universal experience of the divine in the human. Again the spiritualizing of religion imperils the external structures, prized alike by Wittenberg and Rome. The rejection of established forms of worship, though not heresy, offends popular piety and defies public authority.

How seriously this was taken is revealed in the statement of one of the inquisitors, who in the case of Isabel voted for the penalty of death. The arguments which he put into the record were in part traditional. The accused were repeating the heresies of the Beghards and Beguines, of Hus and Wyclif. Another reason, equally current, was that if lèse-majesty against an earthly king is worthy of death how much more lèse-majesty in the form of heresy against the King of kings!

A social note was introduced when the inquisitor linked the Alumbrados to the Communeros, violent revolutionaries, lately devastating the land and only recently crushed. Both, said he, pretended to be reviving the purity of a golden age, the one of the early church, the other of the classical state. If then, the church were lax in dealing with these intransigeants, the Communeros would flare up afresh to the ruin of *La Spangna y el mundo*. "I have tried," said this inquisitor, "to save Isabel on the score of insanity, but of this I can find no trace. My conscience will not allow me to do other than to vote for the penalty of death."

He was overruled by his colleagues and Isabel and Alcaraz were sentenced not to death but to life imprisonment. After some years they were released under surveillance.[37]

## BIBLIOGRAPHY

Bataillon, Marcel, *Erasmo y España* (Mexico City, latest edition 1966).
Longhurst, John, *Luther's Ghost in Spain* (Lawrence, Kansas, 1969), a section on Isabel de la Cruz.
Marquez, Antonio, *Los Alumbrados* (Madrid, 1972).
Nieto, José C., *Juan de Valdes* (Geneva, 1970). In English.
———. "En torno al problema de los alumbrados de Toledo," *Revista española de Theologia* XXXV, Cuad. 1-4 (1975), pp. 77-93. Here he points out very rightly that Alcaraz did not understand unification with God in terms of the negative theology of Dionysius in which all distinctions of truth and error, right and wrong disappear. But this rejection does not require also a denial of the threefold stages of advance in the indwelling of God in man. And the number three is not significant. Alcaraz mentioned among his sources Climacus who posited thirty rungs of the ladder.
Ozment, Steven E., *Homo Spiritualis* (Leiden, 1969) on medieval mysticism.
Ricart, Domingo, *Juan de Valdés* (Spanish, Lawrence, Kansas, 1958) .
The source for the teachings of Isabel de la Cruz and Alcaraz is his *Processo,* which approaches publication in the transcription and annotations of Antonio Marquez. He has kindly supplied me with copies of the Latin summary of the allegations against Isabel, compiled for the briefing of inquisitors who had not attended all of the hearings. Prior to Marquez this document escaped notice. He has given me also copies of a number of briefer letters of Alcaraz to the inquisitors. Mrs. Angela Sanchez Barbudo has supplied me with her transcriptions of Alcaraz' two long letters to the inquisitors, his *Acta Tormento* and the confession of Isabel. The latter has been published by John Longhurst, "La Beata Isabel de la Cruz ante la Inquisition 1524-1529," *Cuadernos de Historia de España* XXV-XXVI (1957), pp. 279-303. The sentence of Alcaraz is published by Manuel Sarrano y Sanz, "Pedro Ruiz de Alcaraz," *Revista de Archivos, Bibliotecas y Museos* VII, I (1903), pp. 1-16

and 126-139. The Latin summary of the allegations against Isabel covers folios 422r to 429r in the *processo*. In the following notes the numbers preceded by the sign * refer to the articles in these allegations. Other references to the *processo* are preceded by fr. and fv. for folio recto and verso.

## NOTES

1. Mt. 10:37.
2. * 119.
3. f.301 and * 125.
4. f.300 and * 127.
5. * 128.
6. John 16:24-25.
7. * 5, 8, 21.
8. f.231, * 23, * 25.
9. * 13, * 107-110.
10. * 124.
11. ** 17, 26, 30-36, 64, 94.
12. ** 30-38, 64, 128.
13. * 117, * 42.
14. ff. 298-9, 302.
15. John 6:62.
16. * 96ff., * 57.
17. Marquez p. 189, the words of another than Isabel.
18. Sanz p. 11, No. 10.
19. ** 36, 43-46, 51, 55-58, 65, 120-21, 136.
20. * 126.
21. * 78.
22. * 92-93.
23. * 84.
24. * 96-97.
25. * 41.
26. * 23. Compare ** 135, 143.
27. II Cor. 3:7 and I Cor. 2:7 King James.
28. * 9-10.
29. f.32r and f.35v.
30. Sanz p. 131 and f.22v.
31. f.235v.
32. f.34v.
33. *32r and f.166r.
34. Sanz p. 12.
35. f.32r.
36. f.325.
37. f.376r - 377v.

# Francisca Hernandez and Francisco Ortiz

Francisca Hernandez was a spiritual leader akin to the Alumbrados. She exerted an astounding influence on a circle of men seriously concerned for religion. A number of Franciscans looked upon this untutored lay woman as a miracle-working saint. Her vogue illustrates how easily an intense religious experience can merge with eroticism. She was active first at Salamanca, then at Valladolid. Beyond this our information is largely drawn from testimony before the Inquisition on the part of one of her devotees, the Franciscan Francisco Ortiz. This brief sketch is really more a biography of him than of her, but at the same time reveals the catastrophic power of a woman to shatter the career of one of the great preachers of his age.

Ortiz thus describes her: "She was small, fair, winsome and charming, so delicate as to frighten her doctor, for frequently she fainted. In her were combined the air of a child and the wisdom and prudence of heaven. . . . Her eyes were a trifle too merry for a saint. . . . She dressed elegantly to show that piety does not consist in a habit." For the same reason she did not become a nun, since she agreed with Erasmus that monasticism is not piety.

Ortiz had been delivered by her from a grievous affliction. During a period of four years he had been so tormented by erotic dreams and frequent emissions that he made an attempt at suicide. Word reached him that through her miraculous power others had been delivered from a like affliction. He sought her out that he might be cured like the woman in the gospel whose issue of blood was staunched by the Savior. At first Francisca refused to see him but yielded to his importunity when he stayed for a week in her area, persistently renewing his request. By the power which issued from her he was healed. He testified:

> When I besought God through his sole mercy to bring me to his holy bride, in the very first conversation she divined all my thoughts. I recognized by a marvelous light that to seek and find God I had no need of any greater truth than that which fell from her lips and that this was the pure grain and substance of the gospel.

And again:

> If to Francisca Hernandez, who counts it as nothing to be servile, despised and ignored of the world, God has given such greatness of soul, such contempt of the world, such joy in persecutions, such wisdom of divine truths, such power of living words which transport the soul and eradicate longing for all that is not of God, such fervor of love, such true and perfect humility, with none of that hypocrisy under which others hide their baseness, such a wealth of spiritual consolations, such pure and excellent chastity, which has delivered me from the debilitating temptations . . . such sincerity and simplicity of a child, together with such authority and heavenly wisdom, must one not say that a person on whom God has conferred such a sea of graces is the acme of all that he can bestow upon a creature? . . . She can be compared to the Mother of God.

Then came word that Francisca had been arrested and thrown into the prison of the Inquisition. The friar then from the pulpit recited the imprecations of the prophets against those who oppressed the children of God and next launched into a diatribe against the Holy Office and the archbishop of Seville. Before the preacher could conclude other Franciscans dragged him from the pulpit and shortly he found himself like Francisca, clapped into the dungeon.

There followed interminable interrogations over the space of
four years. What right had he to emit such a blast? He replied
that he had been constrained by God and his conscience. But
how did he know that the constraint was from God? Why not
from the devil? He appealed to the testimony of the spirit in his
heart, but this, he was reminded, was not evidence in a court
of law. The church does not judge the secrets of the heart. *(De
internis nec ecclesia judicat.)* What concrete evidence could he
produce?

He answered that Francisca had been highly approved by
Cardinal Quinones, the confessor of the Emperor Charles V. She
had made a favorable impression on the Inquisitor General
Adrian, later to be pope. And the Archbishop of Toledo had said
that he would believe all of the claims on her behalf if only she
were a nun. A woman so highly esteemed in such high quarters
might indeed be interrogated but should not be cast into prison.
Furthermore, she had worked miracles. One was his own cure.
Another was that a woman totally unlettered could interpret the
Scriptures with more profundity than the most learned doctors.

The Inquisitor then pried into Ortiz' own orthodoxy, with
hints that he might be Judaizing, since he had some of the blood
of the Jewish conversos. He replied that if there had been anything wrong with his preaching the guardian would not have
permitted him to preach during five successive Lenten seasons.
He had proclaimed only the inexpressible love of God.

He was threatened with torture and replied that it is better to
follow one's conscience than to spare one's body. The Inquisitor
was exasperated by his persistent obstinacy, whereas Ortiz was
irritatingly joyous, unperturbed, serene and peaceable, praying
night and day that God would give him grace to suffer for the
name. He requested only that he might be allowed once a week
to attend Mass, that he might go to confession, and if he were
dying, given the last rites. To this extent only he yielded that if
he were shown the external evidence for Francisca's arrest he
would retract the charges which in his sermon he had levied
against the Inquisition, while still insisting that God had
prompted his protest. He was worried lest this degree of retrac-
tion might be prompted by a desire to escape torture.

He had reason to surmize what the charges against her might be, for he had been asked whether his relations with Francisca were only of the spirit. How often had he been with her? Very infrequently, he said, though near the end on one occasion for about two weeks. Had he slept in her room? No, he had not. Had he given her presents? Yes, a few trinkets; but St. Francis had given his cloak to a beggar. Informed that Francisca was charged with unchastity, he stoutly protested her innocence.

The Inquisition, in the meantime, had been sedulously collecting evidence beyond rumors. A certain Medrano was taxed with having had sexual relations with Francisca. He roundly denied it. Then he was put to the torture and admitted that he had bundled with her and she had enjoyed it, but of carnal union there had been none. Francisca was shown his testimony and flatly denied it. Then, no doubt under threat of torture, she admitted that for the sake of God she had had the same charity for him as he for her and no more. A medical examination proved her to be a virgin. Asked about Ortiz, she replied that on meeting he had sometimes fallen at her feet and kissed the earth but had never exceeded kissing her hand. Another witness testified that once Francisca, sitting at meat next to Ortiz, had let her head fall upon his shoulder.

These depositions were shown to Ortiz, apparently without letting him know that Medrano's confession was elicited by torture and hers by the threat. He collapsed and submitted totally to the judgment of the Inquisition, without ever denying, however, his *belief* that God had required of him the protest. His sentence was relegation to a monastery, with prohibition on saying Mass for two years and preaching for five. Pope Clement VIII showed readiness to restore him to the preaching office in which he had been so eminently effective. But his inner assurance of ability to distinguish between the divine and the demonic had been shattered. How then could he preach? What was left save penitential silence? The hardest feature of the penance was the lack of books.

Francisca, who testified freely against her associates charged with heresy, was released under surveillance.

## BIBLIOGRAPHICAL NOTE

This sketch is based entirely on the admirable book by Angela Selke (Mrs. Barbudo), *El Santo Officio de la Inquisition: Processo de Francisco Ortiz* (Madrid, 1968). She gathers up all that is known about Francisca. This work supersedes Eduard Boehmer, *Franzisca Hernandez und Frai Franzisco Ortiz* (Leipzig, 1865), which, however, is not to be overlooked since it contains informative notes, such as that on the history of the term *recogimiento,* p. 251 and an excursus on the role of women in church history, pp. 48-52.

# Maria Cazalla

The Inquisition never ceased to distrust mysticism. The Spanish mystics survived by avoiding the errors of the Alumbrados condemned in 1525. The Inquisition then turned to the school of Erasmus whose *Dagger of the Christian Soldier* in Spanish translation contained much to disparage the external aids to religion. He did not call for an absolute rejection, but so spiritualized the external as to make it appear superfluous if not detrimental. Take this passage from the *Dagger,* and remember the figure of the ladder dear to Climacus.

> Do you think you will move God by the blood of a bull or by incense? "The sacrifices of God are a broken spirit." You venerate the wood of the cross and have no regard for the mystery of the cross. You fast, refraining from that which does not defile, but you do not refrain from obscene conversation. You adorn a temple of stone, but of what use is this if the temple of the heart is full of abominations? With the mouth you bless, with the heart you curse. You enclose your body in a cell, while your mind wanders over the earth.
>
> Creep not upon the earth, my brother, like an animal. Put on those wings which Plato says are caused to grow on the soul by the ardor of love. Rise above the body to the spirit, from the visible to the invisible, from the letter to the mysti-

cal meaning, from the sensible to the intelligible, from the involved to the simple. Rise as by rungs until you scale the ladder of Jacob. As you draw nigh to the Lord, he will draw nigh unto you. If with all your might you strive to rise above the cloud and clamor of the senses he will descend from light inaccessible and that silence which passes understanding in which not only the tumult of the senses is still, but the images of all intelligible things keep silence.

One can understand why in an atmosphere of paranoia the works of Erasmus were placed in toto on the Index by Pope Paul IV and in part by the Council of Trent.

Among the Spanish Erasmians investigated by the Inquisition only one woman have I been able to discover. The reason may well be that while his piety would attract, his scholarship might repel. He would scoff at looking for a spiritual interpretation of a text which was not so much as to be found in the manuscripts of the Bible. This is not to say that women as a whole had no interest in such questions. Those who did were the products of Renaissance education and there were few such in the toils of the Spanish Inquisition.

The exception was Maria Cazalla. Even she was not concerned for all matters of scholarship, but only for those which ministered to piety. Take the debate about the three Marys, whether Mary Magdalene, Mary the sister of Martha and the woman that was a sinner were one person or three. Maria would leave that to the judgment of Mother Church. And she would have left Erasmus also to the judgment of Mother Church had he at that time been condemned. Seeing that the translation of his work had passed the scrutiny of the Grand Inquisitor, she could say there was not a jot or tittle contrary to the gospels in the works of Erasmus. "I hold what Erasmus holds, because Erasmus holds what Holy Mother Church holds."

The local inquisitors nonetheless pried into her views on Erasmian tenets. Had she scoffed at Aristotle, she was asked, and had she said that Thomas Aquinas, Scotus and the scholastic theology with its sophistications had lost sight of the boy Jesus? She replied that she had not read Aristotle. She had not read

St. Thomas. She had not read Scotus and did not know the meaning of scholastic theology.

But although she disclaimed all knowledge of scholasticism,
she betrayed acquaintance with one of the refinements of scholastic thought, the distinction between approximate merit *(meritum de congruo)* and genuine merit *(meritum de condigno)*. The
teaching was that if men do the best they can with the modicum
of grace which God bestows on all, called prevenient grace, they
will then acquire the lower grade of merit and God will then
bestow extra grace which, if utilized, will result in genuine merit.
Erasmus denied the genuine merit but recognized the lower grade
to account for the passages in the gospel about reward. Maria
denied all merit and in this respect she was actually closer to
Luther. Asked what she thought about him, she said there were
some good things in his earlier writing. "What writing?" "Some
theses," she answered.

Had she, like Erasmus, described many of the observances of
the church as a lapse into Jewish legalism? No, she had not
phrased it in that way, but she had grieved that so many subscribed to bulls of indulgence without paying any attention to
what the pope said about confession and contrition. Had she said
that to die without the sacraments would do no great harm? No,
that she had not said.

Had she said there are loftier themes for contemplation than
the passion of Christ and that it were better to adore his divinity
than his humanity? She didn't remember, but thought she had
said it to a certain friar. "What was his name?" "Oh, it happened
some dozen years ago. I can't remember." (She was adroit at not
remembering incriminations of others.)

Maria was examined also as to whether she was addicted to the
errors of the Alumbrados. She took care to avoid the word Alum-
brado, for she would have been aware of the condemnation of
1525, seeing that her trial ran from 1531-34. By reason of her
association with Isabel de la Cruz and Alcaraz, she could not
escape the charge of being one with them. Had she said that
Isabel had greater authority than St. Paul and the saints? No,
she had not, but she had regarded Isabel and Alcaraz as good
Christians until they were condemned. Thereafter she believed

them to have been seduced by the devil. Had she indulged in the practices with which they were charged? Had she flouted the external acts of devotion: genuflections, making the sign of the cross, bowing at the name of Jesus, standing for the gospel, beating the breast, sprinkling with holy water, the adoration of images? Had she stood bolt upright during the elevation of the host? She answered that she had neglected none of these practices and had taught her sons and her servants to observe them, but she did not believe they had any efficacy of themselves apart from inner devotion.

Had she despised audible prayer? Alcaraz had testified that during prayer he had seen her not moving her lips. To this she replied in the negative. Had she despised sermons? No, but some lacked warmth. Had she condemned the Holy Office? No, she had not. This is an interesting point, because the victims of the Inquisition did not always reject the institution. They agreed that heretics should be suppressed, while insisting that they were not heretics. Had she eaten meat during Lent? Yes, on doctor's orders and with permission of the church.

What of confession and the Eucharist? Did she believe they were of no value, but had nevertheless complied out of deference to public opinion? No, not that, but there had been times when she was not spiritually prepared. After confession she may have recalled something not confessed, and did not feel worthy to come to the altar, but knelt nevertheless rather than give offense to others.

Had she said that if we are filled with the love of God we shall not love our own children more than those of the neighbors? Did she deny natural love? No indeed. She loved her sons and had not neglected them. But the love of parent and child should not be based on blood but on affection. She did not love her sons simply because they were *her* sons, nor did they love her just because she was *their* mother. What about her husband? Had she said that in the act of conjugal union one can be closer to God than in prayer? This was a charge brought several times against Alcaraz and may have been applied to her simply because she was regarded as his disciple. Her answer was a trifle ambiguous.

She had had pleasure with her husband, but it was possible to procreate without carnal pleasure.

A particularly heinous offense was ascribed to her that, though a *woman*, she had dared to preach. Among others Alcaraz had made this accusation, saying that she was arrogant, presumptuous and inspired by self love. She had preached to conventicles, he said. She replied that no conventicles had met in her house. This left open the possibility that they might have met in some other house.

After compiling the charges and her responses the inquisitors decided to put her to the torture. "Why do you need to torture me?" she asked. "I have told the truth and can say no more."

She was taken to the torture chamber and informed that if she were killed, or maimed or bled, the fault would not be theirs. She was ordered to disrobe. "You do this to a woman? I dread more the affront than the pain." When stripped, she cast down her eyes. The torture took two forms. One consisted in tying cords around the thighs and arms with a belt around the waist from which in front cords went up over the shoulders and down to the belt in the back. Tourniquets dug the cords into the flesh at any point of the body.

The other method was the water torture. The victim was bound to a trestle like a ladder with sharp rungs. The head was lower than the feet. The head was clamped immobile and the mouth pried open. Water then trickled from a jar into mouth and nostrils until the victim was nearly suffocated. Then the water was discharged and the process repeated sometimes until as many as eight jars were emptied.

When Maria was strapped, she said, "Even so was Christ lashed to a column." (A familiar depiction in Christian art though not mentioned in the gospels.) As the executioner was about to apply the pressure she exclaimed, "You are trying to make me lie. Do you believe liars?"

One by one the accusations were read to her and after each the inquisitor said, "Tell the truth." And each time she replied, "I have . . ."

"Have you despised the sacraments? Tell the truth."

"I have told the truth."

Torture by Water and the Wheel

"Did you conduct conventicles in your house? Tell the truth."

"I have told the truth."

"Did you refuse to genuflect? Tell the truth."

"I have told the truth."

As the tourniquet was tightened, she screamed, "O Thou who suppliest strength in need, I confess Thee, I adore Thee. Give me strength in my trial." To the constant charges to tell the truth. she cried, "Oh, why do you want me to lie? Saint Stephen, Saint Lorenz, Saints Simon and Jude . . . can the innocent confess what has never been done?" Again she was adjured, "Tell the truth."

"I have, I have, I have told the truth."

"Tell the truth."

"To what I have said I hold. O God to Thee alone will I confess."

The inquisitors said, "It's getting late. We might as well stop." Torment was not to be repeated but could be continued in a later session.

In her case there was none. Since her utterances were deemed to have occasioned scandal, the inquisitors, invoking the name of Christ, passed sentence that she should pay a heavy fine, do public penance and be restricted in her movements. She requested that her husband be informed. She had recanted nothing and incriminated no one.

## BIOGRAPHICAL NOTE

This sketch is drawn entirely from the *Processo contro Maria de Cazalla,* admirably transcribed and edited by Milagros Ortega Emmart, pending publication, on deposit in the library of the University of Massachusetts at Amherst. There is a partial edition by Julio Melagares Marin, *Procedemientos de la Inquisition,* 2 vols. (Madrid, 1896), II, 5-159.

# Marina de Guevara

Lutheranism was more serious than Erasmianism. After all, Erasmus died within the church, but Luther was under excommunication. In the trials of the 1550s the charges against the Lutherans were belief in justification by faith alone, the worthlessness of good works to attain salvation, the denial of purgatory, the reduction of the sacraments to two, the denial of transubstantiation, the serving of the wine in the sacrament to the laity, the definition of the church as the company of the faithful, the assertion that the pope has no more power than the ordinary Christian, the description of the pope as Antichrist and the clergy as Pharisees. So much for Lutheranism. Calvinism also was brought in with the doctrine of predestination and Zwinglianism with the spiritual interpretation of the Lord's Supper. The objections to chants and vestments and the celebration of the Eucharist by the breaking of a loaf suggest the radical sects.

As an example of the trial of a woman charged with Lutheranism, I have taken the *processo* of Marina de Guevara, which ran for sixteen months from May 1558 to September 1559. The period of her interrogations was comparatively short. Years of suspense were frequently a part of the grueling ordeal. The inquisitors deserve credit, however, for thoroughness. All hearings were recorded in detail. The examiners were not captious, though keen to detect evasions.

Marina de Guevara was a nun of somewhat over forty years.

The testimonies about her were mainly from the sisters and the abbess, though also from a man who had visited and spoken through the lattice window. Accounts are given of what took place on occasions when Marina was present. The entire record is revealing of what went on in a convent. One must bear in mind that some of those who testified were themselves under suspicion and were later executed.

Here are samples of the accounts of what occurred when Marina was in attendance.

A certain Catalina de Hortega visited the nunnery and declared openly that the blood of Jesus covers all guilt. There is no purgatory where the sinner continues to make satisfaction, because full satisfaction has already been made by Christ. Confession should be made only to God. When a sister gave Catalina an image of the Infant Jesus, she laughed. "I asked her why she laughed. She asked me why I asked. 'Because,' I said, 'your laughter is altogether out of place.'" Yet this same witness said that she herself had given up vocal prayer. Marina Guevara was present.

Juan Sanchez, whose arrest at Antwerp will later be noticed, brought the sisters a book about the letters of Paul. The witness had concealed it in the infirmary where a group gathered to read and discuss. One was Marina. When Sanchez was told of drops of blood in a cell from flagellation, he said that the castigation of the flesh does not please God and that public penance should be abolished.

Dr. Cazalla came to preach to the sisters and told them that good works do not contribute to salvation but are rather the evidence of salvation. Contrition is not a condition for salvation but a sign of being justified. Abstinences should be dictated by inner feeling. Francisco de Vivero recanted and said that he deserved eternal death for having embraced the teaching of Luther. But Catalina de Alcaraz said fearlessly that the sinner should present to God the blood of Jesus as sole satisfaction for sins which should be bemoaned and confessed. Doña Margareta said we should be joyful at Mass because our sins are forgiven.

"Rejoice. The Son of God has paid the debt." Marina herself
was alleged to have said in the anteroom to one of the sisters
that during the Mass she prayed for the living rather than
the dead.

Then we come to Marina's own testimony. She was of Christian extraction with no trace of Jewish or Moorish blood. Some
three years ago she had subjected herself to such severe penances
that the abbess had enjoined her to spare her health. Then "Catalina de Hortega told me that Christ had paid it all. I rejoiced."
As for Dr. Cazalla, she had believed he was a good Christian. She
was greatly upset on hearing of his arrest. With regard to Sanchez
and the book, she had gained from it great profit till she learned
it was not approved.

Then came interrogations as to the heresies with which she
was charged:

"You say there are only three sacraments."
"No."
"You condemn entirely Jubilees and indulgences."
"Not entirely."
"You reject all oral prayer."
"Not all."
"You say that good works without faith are of no value."
"Not no value."
"You have condemned masses for the dead."
"Not condemned and not neglected."
"You have taught that Lutherans can be sure of their sal-
vation."
"I believe only what Paul says."
"You have called Lutherans brothers."
"I have embraced Hortega."
"You have taught there is no purgatory in the next life."
"I accept the church's teaching."
"Don't you know the church teaches there is a **purgatory for**
those who in this life have not made sufficient satisfaction
for their sins?"
"Yes, of course. I have never believed what the church **does**

not believe. What makes me so weary is that I cannot remember exactly whether I believed there is absolutely no
purgatory or whether it merely seemed to me that there is
not. I was in doubt whether there is or is not. It seemed to
me that it does not exist for those who do the will of God.
Since I was in such doubt I submitted to the opinion of
the church."

"What do you believe now?"

"I believe what the church believes."

"Do you know what the nuns believe about it?"

"No. Talk to them."

"I don't know what Luther has taught about it. Did I say
that at the Mass for the dead it is better to pray for the
living? I don't remember what I said. My memory is weak.
I do think the living are in greater need than the dead. If
you want to condemn me because of my words it is easy. I
express myself poorly. I don't know how to make myself
clear. Have I said that Christians are Pharisees? Yes, including myself. I wish my old Adam were in hell. My memory
is poor and my soul is troubled. For the love of God show
me how I can save my soul and relieve my conscience. I confess that inner works are better than outer. Better than the
castigation of the flesh is the overcoming of pride and anger.
To bring the heart into tune with God is better than audible
prayer. I told one sister not to practice so many penances but
to take refuge in the wounds of Christ and not to trust so
much to the Virgin as to her Son. When a sister was upset
over losing her rosary, I said maybe God had hidden it from
her to keep her from interminable babbling. Some inferred
that I rejected all oral prayer. I have not and do not desire
to depart from the faith of Mother Church. In whatever I
have erred I ask God's pardon and grace."

The abbess petitioned that Marina be allowed to receive the
last sacrament, for she appeared to be on the point of death. The
abbess said her conduct had always been most exemplary and the
sisters testified they would rather pluck out their eyes or delate
against their own parents than to witness against her.

Procession of the Inquisition

A. The standard of the Inquisition.
B. The Dominicans.
C. The heretics who have escaped burning by prior confession.
D. The heretics who have saved themselves by confession after condemnation.
E. The crucifix with its back turned to those to be burned.
F. The heretics to be burned.
G. The remains of those who had died in prison.
H. The Grand Inquisitor.
    Note that those in sections C and D are wearing the apron called the *san benito.*

She was adjudged guilty of heresy and turned over to the temporal arm (that is the civil government because the church abhors the shedding of blood). At the *auto de fé,* when sentence was pronounced, King Philip II and his sister Joanna of Portugal, together with the Crown Prince Carlos, as well as all the court and prelates, sat on the public platform in the square of Valladolil on the 8th of October, 1559.

"Of which," appended the secretary, "I was a witness."

Signed by Julian de Alpuche.

Before turning to a woman who was endorsed by the church in this period, we may draw a few further conclusions from the trials. The examples of Isabel de la Cruz and Francesca Hernandez demonstrate that women enjoyed a wide role in the church so long as not suspected of heresy. And among those who were suspect and condemned, the number of women was about the same as that of men. In the *autos da fé* of March and October 1559, on the first occasion 11 out of 25 were women and on the second out of 16 the women numbered 10. They were from the higher echelons of society.

We find no distinction between men and women in giving testimony with regard to other suspects. Sometimes a woman took the initiative as in the case of Mari Nuñez against Isabela. Those under examination were called upon to name accomplices or mere acquaintances, who then would be subject at least to interrogation. We have the response of Beatriz de Vivero to the demand that she declare her faith. She responded. "I have said that in Christ we have all our treasure and our salvation and one should not worry about works because in God's eyes they are worthless." To whom did she say this? "I said it to Doña Ana, the daughter of the Marquis of Alcanizes and to Doña Francisca de Fonseca, the wife of Alvaro de Lugo and to a young lady, Doña Francisca de Zuniga, the daughter of Antonio de Baeza and also to the Dominican Friar Domingo de Roja."

At the same time women were willing to risk their safety to assist the escape of suspects. Doña Catalina and her mother made possible the flight of Sanchez. Unhappily they did not destroy their correspondence and a letter from him made possible his arrest in Antwerp.

The records give us little intimate glimpses of the share of women in small clandestine gatherings of those in danger of the stake. A woman relates that a Dominican friar was leading the

devotions of several men and women in an upper room awaiting
breakfast. Word came that a woman was downstairs. All looked
dubiously at each other till one vouched for the visitor, who was
admitted.

Friar Domingo gathered the group around the table and,
breaking a loaf, gave to each a portion, saying, "This is my
true body. Take it," and likewise the cup with the words,
"This is my true blood." As we partook, he said, "This is
my body and blood. Take it in remembrance of me." Half
of us were in tears. Then we breakfasted and dispersed. As
I remained sitting with Catalina, I said to her, "Do you
know what I am thinking? I recall how Christ had the supper
with his disciples. Then went out to pray and was seized.
His disciples were offended." And I said to myself, "You will
see how this will end." When we were together in prison, I
reminded her of this. Then Friar Domingo took his leave.

From another source we know that he was garroted.


## BIBLIOGRAPHICAL NOTE

Menendez y Pelayo, *Historia de los Heterodoxes Españoles*, II (Madrid,
    1880), pp. 314ff.
The records of Marina's trial are given in German translation by Ernst
Schäfer, *Geschichte des spanischen Protestantismus und der Inquisition*
(Gütersloh, 1902) as "Der Prozess der Dona Marina de Guevara 1558-
1559" in Vol. 3, pp. 131-257. I have used especially pp. 180-81. The ac-
tivities of the women described at the end of this chapter are from
Vol. 3, pp. 305, 307, 313, 510.

# Teresa of Avila

We have dealt thus far with Spanish women in the toils of the Inquisition. We turn now to one on whom the church conferred sainthood. Her spirituality had much in common with that of the condemned, but she rejected none of the outward observances or formulated dogmas of the church. All these could be retained if infused with the spirit. She is as important as Ignatius Loyola in the resurgence of Catholicism after the secularization of the Renaissance and the shatterings of Protestantism. Her canonization came so speedily that some of her companions were still alive. In the bull which declared her a saint, the pope said she had rendered inestimable services to the church by reforming the Carmelite order, not only for women but also for men and not only for Spain but likewise in other lands.[1]

She was of noble extraction and through her paternal grandfather one quarter Jewish.[2] She had thus, in common with so many of the Alumbrados, the blood of the conversos. Whether this had anything to do with her spiritual orientation may be questioned because St. John of the Cross, so akin to her in piety, was of Spanish blood undiluted.

Her formation was a blend of sainthood and knighthood, of piety and chivalry. In this respect she resembled Loyola. Her introduction to the heroism of the saints came by way of her father, a godly and kindly man who would not own a slave, and to the romances of chivalry by way of her mother, a gentle spirit, married at fifteen, dead at thirty-three, having borne nine children and mothered three more of her husband's. During periods of languor she beguiled herself with the romances of chivalry.

Teresa was first intrigued by the exploits of the saints and at the age of seven conspired with her brother Rodrigo, slightly older, to beg their way to the land of the Moors in order there to have their heads chopped off that they might the sooner see God. Intercepted and returned by an uncle, they set out to be hermits and constructed a hermitage of pebbles, which fell down. Such failures may have inclined her the more to relish the adventures of knighthood recounted in the books left carelessly about by her mother to the father's high displeasure. The children surreptitiously gorged on the forbidden fruit and Teresa became a wicked woman. She used perfume. Her mother died when she was only fourteen and Teresa besought the Virgin Mary to be henceforth her mother. When an older half sister married and left the home, the father, feeling that she needed motherly care, placed her in a convent. In time, to his distress, she was disposed to take the vows. Should she not wait till after his death? But she was insistent and he became reconciled. She was then twenty.[3]

Now began a quarter of a century of wrestling with the angel, questing to experience the presence of God, to be utterly united with him in the bond of unfeigned love. The way was tortuous with risings and fallings in the course of a steady progression. She delineated the stages by the analogy of the modes of filling the cisterns.[4] The first was laboriously to draw water from a well with a bucket and a rope. The next was to employ one of those little Moorish windlasses in use on every Castillian farm. This was easier than the first and harder than the third which was to dip a pan into a living stream and the water would be purer than in any well. The fourth stage was to lay out vessels in the open to catch the rain coming down from above. The first three involved degrees of human effort. The last was solely the gift of God.

Her fourfold scheme is not that of the traditional demarcation of the stations along the mystic way of purification, illumination and unification. She was familiar with the pattern but like other mystics did not relish geometrical precision. Yet her delineation of her spiritual struggles corresponds very well with the threefold course.

The first is purification. It affects the body and even more the soul and spirit which are not to be distinguished. In the case of the body, the object is by disciplined living to subdue the lusts of the flesh, the gratification of passion, the coddlings of comfort. The extreme device is the mortification of the flesh through self-inflicted pain, the wearing of hair shirts, flagellation, fasting.

Teresa did not absolutely eschew such methods and used them herself to a degree but mortifications were not of themselves an end in her eyes and should not be taken to excess to the detriment of health. The body is indeed the cage of the spirit, but the cage should be kept in good order. When her brother, a widower with two sons, asked her whether he should become a monk, the answer was, "No. Look after your boys." Well, what then would she think of his wearing a hair shirt? "Not oftener than twice a week," she answered, "And only during the day. Do not sleep in it and if it goes all round the body put a linen cloth over the belly. God prefers health and obedience to your penances. Get enough sleep and enough food. What is the point of mortification? The real point is the love of God." [5]

There are other ways of controlling the body than by the infliction of pain. One is simple living. Wear used clothes, worn and patched but neat, not smelling of sweat.[6] Wear sackcloth or a horse blanket, no shoes or only peasant sandles. Be abstemious in eating and drinking. If rich, live as if poor.[7] For St. Francis, Lady Poverty gave liberation from the distractions and contentions of possessions. For Teresa she was closer to mortification to curb the selfish cravings of the natural man.[8]

Purification of the spirit is vastly more important than of the flesh and more difficult, for it means the overcoming of self-love, the readiness in utter obedience to follow what one deems to be the commands of God. Along with love, humility is here the cardinal virtue. Humility is better than fasts.[9]. It is not a false modesty.[10] When Teresa heard someone call her a saint, she ejaculated, "I have been told I am good looking and I have not demurred. I have been told I'm brilliant and I have not contradicted, but a saint—oh, no." [11] She would have no titles to set her

off from others and as a prioress would not be called reverend.[12]
Humility welcomes criticism [13] and does not defend itself even
against false accusations,[14] but if someone else were maligned
Teresa was quick with the poignard. The Samaritan woman was
her especial favorite because when Jesus reminded her of her
loose life, she did not bristle but called him a prophet.[15] Harbor
no restentment [16] and be not outraged by an injustice. Once
Teresa, in a coarse mantle, was jammed in a crowd in a church.
A peasant woman accused her of stealing her clog and with the
other gave her a pummeling. Teresa laughed at the error.[17]

Illumination is the second stage in the sequence of the mystic
way, but Teresa made no sharp demarcations. She talks much of
prayer and meditation which both purge and enlighten. Prayer
involves human effort as "the hart pants after the water
brooks." [18] Illumination is the response to him who "sends forth
his light and his truth."[19] The approach to God is always open.
There is no need to make an appointment, no protocol in heaven,
no need for a Lord High Chamberlain to usher one into the presence of the King of kings. Prayer is  efficacious in calming the
spirit, in affecting the course of nature, sometimes averting disasters, and especially in the affairs of men whether in this life
or the next.[20]

Prayer is of two kinds, vocal and mental. The vocal is commonly the use of a liturgical form or any verbalization. Mental
prayer is more a matter of mood and is scarcely to be distinguished from meditation.[21] And this also takes two forms, the
ones we have already noted in the case of Alcaraz: relaxation
*(dexamiento)* and concentration *(recogimiento)*.[22] Teresa preferred the latter and centered her meditation on the humanity
of Christ. In this she resembled Loyola who in his *Spiritual Exercises* demanded intense and exclusive concentration upon one
episode after another, strictly one at a time.[23]

In the life of Christ she had a penchant for scenes involving
women, the Samaritan woman,[24] as just noted, and often Mary
and Martha.[25] Of course, the sufferings of Christ were not overlooked. When she was grieving over the wounds from the crown
of thorns, he appeared to her and said that these were not so
grievous as the wounds daily inflicted.[26] She confessed that in the

beginning she had had great difficulty in achieving concentration.[27]

The third station of the mystic ascent was unification. For Teresa it included two subdivisions, communion and union. Both were solely the work of God. Communion came through visions. The spirits appeared of her father and mother, St. Claire, the Virgin, Joseph and the Trinity, but most frequently Christ.[28] Sometimes she had visions termed "intellectual," in which there was only the sense of a presence. Such a vision might last for a year.[29] Other visions were so vivid that she tried to detect the color of Christ's eyes [30] and so auditory as to become long conversations. Christ could never be summoned by rubbing on some Aladdin's lamp, but whenever she was in need he was invariably there. She could have sung the Protestant hymn, "He walks with me and he talks with me."

One who is a stranger to such experiences is prone to think of her as "trailing clouds of glory" from her heavenly home and living in a world where fact and fancy blend. How reassuring she found these visitations! Christ brought her consolation, encouragement, counsel and command. He told her precisely what she was to do. There was no call for the courage of an Abraham who "went out not knowing whither he went." Yet Teresa was no child. *If* it were Christ who spoke, her assurance was complete, but was it Christ after all? Well she knew that the devil could appear in the guise of the Redeemer. How could she tell? She asked her confessor, who told her to make the sign of the cross which would avaunt the evil one. She feared to be crossing every second and instead brought along a crucifix. When Christ next appeared she apologized for this mark of distrust. He assured her that it was quite all right because she did it out of obedience.[31]

Her ultimate test for the supernatural source of these experiences was to be found in the fruits of the spirit. If they made her more disinterested, sympathetic, tender and loving then they were of God.[32] A modern psychologist might suspect that she put into the mouth of Christ precisely that which she wanted him to say. This is correct only if one remembers that she wanted him to say what she did not want him to say. There was in her subconscious a conflict between desire and conscience. Not what she craved on the top level of the subconscious but what she felt she ought to crave at the deepest level was what Christ would enjoin. Once, for example, when she was engaged in founding new monasteries she was called to return to the convent of the Incarnation as prioress. She did not want to leave what she was doing. Christ said "Go." And she went in joyous obedience.[33]

Along with communion came union. This was an experience of rapture, ecstasy, trance. Sometimes it came tumultuously, irresistibly, devastatingly with physical accompaniments such as temporary paralysis. The senses are suspended, the memory void, the imagination benumbed. The experience may last no longer than the saying of an Ave Maria. The transports of joy exceed all the delights of entrancing vistas of woods and waters. The rapture is indescribable and incommunicable. This is what "eye hath not seen, ear hath not heard, neither hath it entered into the heart of man."[34] One can talk only of inebriation, intoxication, madness. The fool in Christ is drunk with God.[35] Moses could not describe what he had experienced before the burning bush. He could deliver to the children of Israel only those words which the Lord placed in his mouth.[36]

In the mystical experience there is such a union of man with God that man may be said to have become God, for God became man in order that man might become God. The incarnation is to a degree universalized. This does not mean, of course, that man becomes the Lord God Omnipotent. Nor does it mean that the individual is swallowed up in the abyss of being. The union is more nearly that of the will.[37] A favorite figure with the mystics was that of a candle burning in the sunlight. Because of the greater brilliance the flame of the candle is not seen. The candle remains, however, an individual candle. The nature of the union is expressed by various figures, a number of which appear in the writings of Teresa. The union is like the conjunction of fire and flame, like the merging of rain water with that of a spring, the running together of molten wax from two candles, the blending of lights coming in through two windows.[38] There is that of God in man.

The sense is best expressed in prayers of exultation. Teresa exclaims:

O King of glory, Lord of Lords, Emperor of Emperors, holy of the holiest, power above all powers, wisdom above all wisdoms. Truth itself art Thou and riches. Of Thy reign there is no end. Thy perfections cease not. Infinite are they above all understanding, a bottomless ocean of wonders, a loveliness comprising all beauties and strength. O that I had the tongue to declare what here below cannot be known save for the lineaments in a measure of him who is our Lord and peace.[39]

Or take the first stanza of her poem:

I live, yet live not in me.
I crave another life on high.
I die because I cannot die.[40]

Such intense exaltations were not of long duration and in between would come long periods of drought, dryness, aridity, melancholy, the dark night of the soul.[41] She knew from experience and offered prescriptions: continuance in prayer, diverting conversation, a stroll in the woods, care for the body.[42] This last injunction was particularly timely because the rhythms of the spirit were paralleled by those of the body. She had known alternations of physical debility and vitality. Once she had been taken for dead and for three years was a paralytic. Often she vomited in the morning and could not take food until midday.[43] Was there any correlation and causal connection between the physical and spiritual oscillations? To a degree she observed it [44] and ascribed a certain woman's depressions to "a strong imagination, a disordered body and the devil." [45] Trance might cause a shock.[46] Raptures brought rather improvement in health.[47]

Now after twenty-five years in the enclosure of the Incarnation, she became a "gadabout," founding throughout Castille and Andalusia new monasteries where women and men could dwell in holy seclusion. Why such a change? It was not as abrupt as may appear. She maintained always that the contemplative and the active lives should be conjoined. Jesus chided Martha for complaining of Mary but did not tell her to go and join her sister. In that case there would have been no dinner.[48] When

Teresa was at the Incarnation she was happy to spend hours
sweeping [49] and, though she resented interruption in her devotions by taking time to eat,[50] she stood ready to drop all at the
call of pots and pans.[51] And if, during her evening prayers, she
heard a sister groping for her cell, Teresa would hasten to bring
a candle.[52]

Besides, Teresa did not regard her prayers as inactive and in-
operative. The defenders of the church, the preachers, scholars
and administrators in order to roll back the ravages of the Lutherans, needed to have their hands upheld by a humble little
woman.[53] And beyond the grave also her intercessions were potent. There was a man, who having been marvelously helpful in
enabling her to start a new foundation, died unable to make confession because of a loss of speech. Teresa entreated the Lord
Jesus to excuse him from purgatory and take him straight to
heaven. Jesus thought this inappropriate but promised to release
the man after the first mass had been said in the new foundation.
Thereupon the liberated soul appeared in a vision to tender his
most heartfelt gratitude.[54]

But if Teresa was so powerful with her prayers why the shift
to the new mode of activity? The answer is obedience. She became acquainted with the primitive rule of the Carmelites in
accord with the word of Christ to sell all and his example of
having nowhere to lay his head. Teresa may have been unaware
that she was picking up a theme agitated for centuries by the
Franciscans and being revived in her own day in Italy by the
Capuchins. In utter devotion to Lady Poverty they would not
gather into barns, wear soft raiment or put on shoes to traverse
the rough roads of Italy. Teresa would do the like for Spain.

She must first examine herself as to whether she was living up
to the rule. It forbade possessions and she possessed images of
Jesus, Mary and the saints. Were they not property in violation
of the rule? She thought a picture on a piece of paper would not
be an infringement. Her confessor told her that images of the
Holy Family and the saints were exempt from the rule. She was
greatly relieved for she was sure that the poor Lutherans in
giving up images were on the way to perdition.[55]

Teresa now resolved to establish a new foundation. She was

quite sure that the one hundred and eighty sisters at the Incarnation abbey would not be converted overnight to such rigor. Consequently with only two sisters she set out to establish a new house. Her own sister greatly helped by providing an abode. Then this frail figure, clad in sackcloth or a horseblanket, in peasant footwear, would move into a dilapidated hut and over night convert it into a chapel with an altar to the Son of God. Time after time she travelled in covered wagons, through torrid heat and congealing cold, over roads dusty, muddy or frozen, over fords in ferries where the cable might break and send the scow careening over rapids until beached on the sandbank.[56]

Her foundations were all dedicated to Saint Joseph because Mary would certainly have been pleased to see him given recognition for all the chores he did on her behalf.[57] Teresa had evidently been affected by a new style in the depictions of Joseph holding a lantern, kindling a fire, boiling soup and drying diapers. But she did not originate the cult of Joseph.

The hardships of travel were the least of her trials. Obedience was her watchword, but to whom? To Christ, of course, but on earth to whom? to the king? to the pope? Both desired reform in Spain. Philip II and the popes of the Counter-reformation shared the same aims but were at odds as to who should take the lead. The saying was "There is no pope in Spain." [58] A pattern had been developing over the centuries of control of the church by the crown, a comparative independence from Rome and undeviating orthodoxy. The institution of the Spanish Inquisition was more a royal than papal affair.

The crown and the tiara were not the only ones at odds. The general of the Carmelites, invariably an Italian, resident in Italy, clashed with the provincial in Spain. The provincial's jurisdiction might overlap with that of the bishop and he must consult the mayors and town councils when it came to permission for the introduction of more holy beggars. The municipal authorities might be sustained or reversed by the governor.

In dealing with all these Teresa could count on stout support from three men. The first was King Philip II. She wrote to him.[59] She went to Madrid and called on him. He allowed her to kiss his hand.[60] Her two great lieutenants were St. John of the Cross and Gracian. The first was a marvelous director of souls. Gracian, just under thirty, son of the king's secretary, might have become a distinguished diplomat had he not chosen to join the saints in rags.[61] He was eminently qualified to deal with the chiefs of church and state.

The foundations might have been established more smoothly had they been only for women. But when Gracian moved to extend the reform to men, terror struck the unreformed male Carmelites lest the movement should so far spread as to engulf them also. They were known as the followers of the Mitigated Rule, and also as the Calced, that is the shod, as over against the Discalced, the shoeless. Teresa called the Calced the Grasshoppers and her Discalced the Butterflies.[62]

As the tension mounted the general of the Carmelites, the Italian Rubeo, decided to break the traditional practice and go to Spain himself. He came not too favorably disposed toward the reformers but was won over by Teresa. As for the mayor and the governor, she confronted them in person with equal irresistibility.

But now the Calced took fright and were favored when a new papal nuncio, named Sega, came to Spain determined to assert his authority and to demand absolute allegiance from Teresa, John of the Cross and Gracian. Teresa he described as "a restless, gadabout, disobedient, contumacious woman who promulgates pernicious doctrine under pretense of devotion. She leaves her cloisters against the orders of her superiors contrary to the decrees of the Council of Trent. She is ambitious and teaches theology as if she were a doctor of the Church in spite of St. Paul's prohibition." [63] As for Gracian, Sega would return to Rome if this defier of his jurisdiction were not burned.[64]

This was not idle talk. John of the Cross was kidnapped and for nine months imprisoned with treatment more harsh than any inflicted by the Inquisition. Solitary, hungry, amid stenches, with no light save through a small aperture in the ceiling, he was beaten daily.[65] Gracian carried hard boiled eggs in the shell to forefend poisoning.[66] Teresa hid. She appealed to Philip II who resisted the papal nuncio but could not secure the release of John of the Cross, for who knew where he was? He proved himself to be no mere transcendental dreamer, for with great ingenuity he contrived to loosen the screws in the lock and having made a rope from shreds of his bedclothes he let himself out of a window. Gracian was briefly imprisoned. At last the pope agreed to separate the Carmelites into two provinces, the Calced and the Discalced, each with its own provincial. The Butterflies were free from the Grasshoppers.[67]

Teresa's work was now essentially done. She lived two more years and established two more foundations, making fifteen in all. One marvels that this visionary was so astonishingly endowed with that uncommon quality commonly called common sense. She was amused by petty legalists as to obedience. Once she was standing with a prioress on the edge of a pool with a sister nearby. Teresa said to the prioress, "What would you think if I were to tell that sister to jump in the pool?" The girl overheard and jumped.[68] Another nun came to the prioress for her to admire a lovely worm. "O yes," smiled the prioress, "Why don't you cook it and have it for supper?" And she went off and did (at any rate the cooking).[69]

Teresa did not approve of the practice of sisters who would slap and pinch each other to provide exercise in patience.[70] And she was tart with a worrywart who had come with her into a rough neighborhood to start a foundation. As the two were sleeping together the companion fidgeted. "What's the matter with you?" asked Teresa. "I was thinking," she answered, "how dreadful it would be if I died suddenly during the night and left you to fend for yourself." "I'll take that on when it comes," responded Teresa. "Go to sleep." [71] She was quite able to twit and to be twitted. To a friend she wrote, "You find it as hard to write a long letter as I a short." [72] She asked Gracian to suggest for her a mortification. He replied, "Have your picture painted." [73]

One of the most attractive aspects of her common sense is the recognition of human varieties. We are not all like the Apostle Paul.[74] We need not all be angels to pray, "Hallowed be thy name." [75] Some experience aridities at the beginning and some at the end of the spiritual pilgrimage.[76] In her own devotions she had experienced variant moods.[77] Some persons are capable of mortifications and some are not.[78] When against her inclination she was made prioress at the Incarnation a minority were disgruntled fearing that she would impose on them her austerities. She did not, for mortifications are worthless if not wished.[79] Let none be envious or slack because endowed with lesser gifts. She herself had not been granted the gift of song.[80] If we cannot mount up with wings as eagles let us not shuffle like a hobbled hen.[81]

For all her mortifications she did not decline to enjoy life's simple joys. "I loved," she wrote, "to look upon field, stream and flowers. In them I saw traces of the Creator." [82] In one of her foundations she had a cell looking out upon a river. Lying in bed she found solace in watching its flow.[83] She took delight in a little girl at the nunnery. Of her she wrote: "The little creature's wits are extraordinary. She has a few poor little statues of some shepherds, some nuns, and a figure of our Lady, and not a feast day comes around, but she invents some little scene with them: she composes verses, and sings them to us so well and to such a pretty tune that we are astonished." [84] Teresa herself talked to images of Jesus and Mary as if they were dolls [85] and decorated the statuettes of the saints with flowers.[86]

Since Teresa's interiorization of religion resembled that of the Alumbrados investigation by the Inquisition was to be expected. When word of this came to her, she could not refrain from laughing that she should be suspect, despite her utter devotion to the doctrine and rules of the church. She rejected neither hell nor purgatory, and, as for the Trinity, would venture no opinion on points she did not understand. The external aids to religion, though not of the essence, were not to be abandoned: images, rosaries, liturgical prayers, genuflections and the like. Holy water differs from ordinary water by reason of the ordinance of the church, and Teresa found it very effectual. Investigations for a full decade left her unperturbed, save for the fear of impediment to her work. She was at length completely vindicated.[87]

A paramount question concerning the role of women in the religious movements of the sixteenth century is what Teresa herself thought about her role. No woman thus far examined had as much to say on this point as she. This is partly because she wrote so much. Her meditations for her sisters and daughters often contain asides about their sex. The greater part of her letters are to men. This was inevitable because during the twenty-five years in the nunnery of the Incarnation she had no occasion to address letters to the sisters. When, however, she emerged as the foundress of new houses her dealings with officials were entirely with men. The popes were men as were the kings, the generals and provincials of the order, the bishops, mayors and governors. And what is more significant for her spiritual development, all of her confessors were men.

In assessing her comments one needs to have in mind her situation. In Spain, as elsewhere throughout Europe, women did not enjoy an equal status.[88] For wives, though not for husbands, adultery was a crime. Women did, indeed, have property rights, but in the field of education they were seldom taught more than to read and write. The ideal of humanist education for women voiced by Erasmus was for a time in vogue but declined as his star was eclipsed. The unmarried woman had little opportunity for an independent career. She might be a prostitute, a nun or a housekeeper and servant. In literary circles there were defenders as well as detractors of women. Probably the most invidious detractors were the clergy because they held to the myth of the fall of man through Eve and enforced the injunction of the Apostle Paul that women should be silent in church and not too voluble anywhere.[89] Ecclesiastes might refer to women as *mujeres y ydiotas,* women and blockheads. The word *ydiota* in Spanish does not mean idiot, but rather simply unlettered, but the tone is very derogatory. Teresa's project of founding new monasteries was mocked as a piece of women's foolishness.[90]

The inferior status of women was, of course, an undeniable fact. Teresa took note of the double standard as to chastity.[91] To a degree she accepted also the current belief in the inferiority of women. Their frailties, she said, expose them especially to the wiles of Satan.[92] Girls are harder to teach than boys.[93] Weak and irresolute women, like Teresa herself, need some consolations that they may weather the tribulations which God chooses to impose.[94] Being a woman is enough to deflate one's sails without being also a wicked woman [95] (as Teresa esteemed herself to be).

Sometimes the assumed weakness of women was used as a foil to ward off inquisitorial prying into theological niceties. How could a poor unlettered woman be expected to understand such questions? [96] She did not pretend to fathom all the aspects of the Trinity [97] but because of such incapacity should women be deprived of the riches of the Lord? [98]

In some respects, however, Teresa insisted on the superiority of women. The favors of the Lord are more often granted to them. "Peter Alcantara said this and my experience confirms it. 'Women,' he said, 'make greater progress on the path to perfection than men.' He gave excellent reasons for this which there is no need to repeat." [99] (Too bad!) "But how about the injunction of the Apostle Paul that women should keep silent in church?" "Don't go by one text only." [100] Women are more loving than men and have other gifts of service to the community. They take time to share their concerns and just to chitchat, and they form close intimacies.[101]

Whatever the weakness of women it gave the Lord an opportunity to exhibit his power in working wonders through infirm vessels. Here is a passage which blends the status of women, the weakness of women and the Lord's doing. Teresa tells of a woman who is grieved over the deficiency of her sex and envies those who are free to lift up their voices proclaiming the greatness of the Lord of Hosts.

> Poor little fettered butterfly who cannot fly where she will! Have pity on her, O Lord, that she may be able to accomplish something for thy honor and glory. Look not upon her meagre desert and the lowliness of her sex. Thou, O Lord, canst repel the ocean and open the Jordan that the children of Israel may pass through. Show forth thy power in this thy creature, weak and womanly, that all may see it is not of her and give to thee the glory.[102]

There was another advantage which she would never have thought to adduce that women have a way with men by virtue of feminine graces. One may surmise that Rubeo, the general of

the Carmelites, when he came to Spain ill disposed to her reform, was won over by her earnestness in part, but also perhaps by a disarming smile from beneath the hood of a horse
blanket with bare toes peeking from below.

But though the friendships of Teresa with men were intimate, there is no trace of the erotic in her deportment or writing. Her commentary on the first verse of the Song of Solomon,
"O that you would kiss me with the kisses of your lips," is very
different from that of St. Bernard who treats the reference to the
lips as an expression of passionate desire. She asks, as he did,
"Why the lips?" And answers, "I don't know. It signifies a very
great love." [103] She used, of course, some of the bridal imagery
of the New Testament. The Lord Jesus was her groom and
brought to her as an engagement ring a nail (from his cross).[104]

Her piety is well epitomized in a poem often attributed to her
though quite possibly anonymous.[105]

I love thee not, my God, for heaven's reward.
I fear thee not for hell's eternal flame.
Were there no hell I'd love thee just the same.
Were there no hell still would I fear thee, Lord.

I'm moved to see thy lacerated side.
I'm moved to look when hands and feet are nailed.
I'm moved to see thy body so impaled.
To look upon thee mocked and crucified.

## BIBLIOGRAPHY

*Obras Completas* (abbr. *Ob.*) ed. Efren de la Madre de Dios y Otger
Steggink, 2d ed. (Madrid, 1967). This edition is not quite complete as
to the letters. Some I have used in the English translation *The Letters
of Saint Teresa,* 4 vol. (London, 1919-1929). Abbr. *Lett.* The notes
and introductions are very useful.

Ribera's life has been available to me only in a French translation:
*Vie de Sainte Térèse* par François de Ribera (Paris, 1884).

Several of Teresa's works are available in English separately. The chapters correspond to the *Obras* in number but not the subdivisions. Her
autobiography *The Life of St. Teresa of Jesus* was translated by David
Lewis (London, 1904).

*The Interior Castle* (the *Moradas*) (London, 1912).

The Book of Foundations, translated by John Dalton (London, 1860).
The Way of Perfection (Camino), translated by Alice Alexander (West-
minster, Maryland, 1946) reads delightfully but is difficult to check
with the Spanish because readings have been taken from different
manuscripts.
Lovet, Lady and Benson, R. H. *The Life of Saint Teresa* (London,
1912), sparsely documented and hagiographic.
Crisôgondo de Jesús, *Santa Teresa de Jesús* (Barcelona, 1942), documented.
Underhill, Evelyn, *Mysticism* (London, 1930), illuminating.
Martinez, Enrique Llamas, *Santa Teresa de Jesús y la Inquisition
Española* (Madrid, 1972), detailed.
Villanueva, Francisco Márquez, "Santa Teresa y el Linaje," pp. 139-202
in "Espiritualidad y Literatura en el Siglo XVI," *Hombres, Hechos
e Ideas*, XVI (Madrid, 1968). Her partial *converso* lineage.

# NOTES
* denotes section or paragraph.

1. R I, p. v.
2. *Ob.* introduction p. 1.
3. Autobiography Ob. p. 59ff. and R.
4. *Ob.* p. 59 * 7.
5. *Ob.* pp. 852f; 178 * 9; p. 848. *Lett.* II, pp. 253-4, cf. p. 242. Camino
   XI. *Ob.* p 230 * 17, p. 380-3.
6. *R* II, p. 268.
7. *R* II, p. 329, cf. pp. 268, 329.
8. *R* II. xvi. p. 235.
9. *Ob.* p. 235.
10. *Ob.* p. 241.
11. Too good not to be true. Note lost.
12. *Lett.* IV, p. 142.
13. *R* II, p. 250.
14. *Ob.* p. 238.
15. *Ob.* p. 360 * 7.
16. *Ob.* ch. XI, p. 194 f.
17. *R* II, p. 254.
18. *Ps.* 42:1.
19. *Ps.* 43:3.
20. *Ob.* p. 169, * 6.
21. Camino ch. XXXVII-XLI, *Ob.* 264-72.
    *R* II, p. 133.
22. *Ob.* p. 388 * 4.
23. *Ob.* p. 281, * 3.
24. *Ob.* p. 360 * 7.
25. *Ob.* pp. 238, 246.

26. *R* I, p. 221.
27. *Ob.* p. 36 * 9.
28. Parents, *Ob.* p. 171 * 1; St. Claire, Joseph. *Ob.* p. 150. Mary *Ob.* pp. 464, 469. Trinity *Ob.* pp. 464, 482, *R* II, pp. 69, 72, 76. Christ *Ob.* p. 427 * 3, p 118 * 2. and passim.
29. *Ob.* pp. 426-7, 431.
30. *Ob.* 128 * 2.
31. *R* I, p. 65, *Ob.* p. 129.
32. *Ob.* p. 431.
33. *Ob.* p. 560 * 3.
34. I Cor. 2:9. King James.
35. Suspensions: *Ob.* p. 63 * 5, p. 414, pp. 513, 605 * 36. Tumultuous *Ob.* p. 434. Inebriation *Ob.* p. 532 * 15, *Ob.* p. 125 * 9.
36. *Ob.* p. 414 * 5.
37. *Ob.* p. 399.
38. *Ob.* p. 441 * 6, R II, p. 62.
39. *Ob.* p. 266 * 6.
40. *Ob.* p. 499.
41. Fundaciones VII is devoted to Melancholia. *Ob.* 535 ff.
42. *Ob.* p. 62 * 7; cf. p. 421 * 9; p. 720 * 4; *R* II, p. 142.
43. *Ob.* p. 41 * 2; p. 46, * 11.
44. *Ob.* p. 61 * 16.
45. *Ob.* p. 804; *Lett.* II, 108.
46. *Ob.* p. 91 * 9.
47. *Ob.* p. 455 * 31, cf. p. 94 * 21.
48. *Ob.* p. 246 * 5.
49. *Ob.* p. 35 * 2.
50. *Ob.* 457 * 6.
51. *Ob.* 528 * 8.
52. *R* II, p. 194.
53. *Ob.* p. 197 * 2.
54. *Ob.* p. 54 * 2.
55. Fundaciones *Ob.* p. 514 ff. & R.
56. *Ob.* p. 483.
57. *Ob.* pp. 42-43.
58. Otger Steggink, *La Reforma del Carmel Español* (Rome, 1965) p. 10. Excellent on the jurisdictions.
59. *Ob.* p. 737, no. 84.
60. *Lett.* III, p. 17.
61. *Lett.* I, p. 192 note.
62. *Ob.* p. 815 * 3.
63. *Lett.* III, pp. 157-8.
64. *Lett.* III, p. 109
65. Crisogono de Jesus, *Life of St. John of the Cross* (Ld., 1958).
66. *Lett.* I p. 270.
67. *Ob.* p. 612 * 30.

68. *Ob.* p. 558 * 3.
69. *Ob.* p. 566 * 12.
70. *Ob.* p. 808 * 13.
71. *Ob.* p. 568 * 5.
72. *Ob.* p. 77 * 12.
73. *Lett.* II, p. 137 note.
74. *Ob.* p. 352 * 3, cf. pp. 245, 288.
75. *Ob.* p. 288.
76. *R* II, p. 146 * 16.
77. *Ob.* p. 452.
78. *Ob.* 565.
79. Crisogono, pp. 71-74.
80. *Ob.* p. 142 * 23.
81. *Ob.* p. 180 * 12.
82. *Ob.* p. 53 * 5.
83. *Ob.* p. 56.
84. *Lett.* II, p. 211.
85. *R* II, p. 165.
86. *R* II, p. 169.
87. *Ob.* pp. 148-9 and Martinez.
88. Melveena McKendrick, *Woman and Society in the Spanish Drama of the Golden Age* (Cambridge, Eng., 1974).
89. Antonio Marquez, *Los Alumbrados* (Madrid, 1972). p. 142.
90. *Ob.* p. 147.
91. *Ob.* p. 385 * 5.
92. *Ob.* p. 107.
93. *Ob.* 706, no. 50.
94. *Ob.* p. 61.
95. *Ob.* p. 57 * 8.
96. *Ob.* p. 59.
97. *Ob.* p. 482 * 5.
98. *Ob.* 336 * 9.
99. *Ob.* p. 186 * 8.
100. *Ob.* p. 463 * 16a.
101. *Ob.* pp. 208-9 * 3.
102. *Ob.* p. 420.
103. *Ob.* pp. 336-7.
104. *R* II, p. 175.
105. Guillermo Diaz-Plaja, *Antologia Mayor de la Literatura Española II Renacimiento* (Barcelona etc. 1958), p. 1016.

# PORTUGAL

# Luisa Sigea
## (1522-1560)

Luisa Sigea, our choice for Portugal, was not exactly Portuguese, nor exactly a reformer. Her father came from France, attended the university of Alcalá and there learned Latin, Greek and Hebrew. He married a woman of the Spanish nobility. For support he tutored in the court of the governor of Toledo, who, having placed himself at the head of the revolting Communeros, with their failure lost his head. His widow fled to Portugal and Sigea went with her and gave her support for nine years. In the meantime he became the father of two sons and two daughters whom he instructed in all the languages at his command and employed for Luisa a tutor in Arabic and Syriac. She is said to have been able to talk in a measure in these tongues before she could read, which is likely enough if they were spoken to her. Before the age of twenty she was renowned as a female prodigy, who a little later addressed Pope Paul III in a letter in five tongues. He had to get help to reply in kind.

Luisa found employment as tutor to the infanta, Maria of the royal court of Portugal. The life there nauseated her, with all of the ambition, vanity, jealousy and the stilted cleverness of repartee. She married and left the court to enjoy a tranquil retreat. But the stipend ceased. For a time help came through service to Maria of Hungary, then regent of the Netherlands (a sketch of her follows in this volume). On the abdication of her brother, the Emperor Charles V in 1555, Maria retired with him to Spain and there died after three years. Help from that source came to an end.

Luisa then tried to secure employment for her husband by way of a petition to Philip II. No answer! When Philip married a French princess access to her was obtained through the French ambassador and another request presented. No answer! Then a plea to Don Carlos, the Spanish heir apparent. He was a degenerate. No answer!

Broken in spirit Luisa wrote to a friend.

> You have written me a letter which no one else could write and I would not have desired from any other. It exudes the fragrance of a life unspotted, which I would inhale were I not so spoiled by the stench of the human as to be incapable of the divine and must cry with Jeremiah, "Death has come into our windows." [1] Were I not so encompassed by death as scarcely to know the meaning of life, enveloped in darkness and filled with horror by light; were I not torpid, enervated, with no lust for learning, like a weary invalid for whom the very curatives have become insipid. If I have not responded, the cause is shame and remorse for my indolence. I am undeserving of your praise, though eager for your counsel. Help me with your words and guidance. I have not strength for the path of life. [2]

A few weeks after the writing of this letter she was claimed by death. We have from her pen a work extant in only one copy, a dialog between two women, Blésilla, defending the contemplative life, and Flaminia the active. An old debate this was indeed, but there is here a different flavor because Luisa combines the humanist craving for a sylvan glade "far from the madding crowd's ignoble strife," where elect spirits can hold converse with each other and the immortal dead. This she combines with the revival of Catholic piety in prayer, meditation and ecstasy. Luisa brings to mind the sonnets of lamentation of Vittoria Colonna, whose work she knew and admired and the weariness of Marguerite of Navarre with all the trivial vanities of the courts of kings. There is also the same longing for learning, light, wisdom and the vision of God. She blends, like the humanists, the strains of classical antiquity, especially of the moralists, Plato, Plutarch, Cicero and Seneca, together with the Torah, the prophets, the psalms and the canticles, with the gospels and Paul with the fathers, Chrysostom, Ambrose, Augustine, Cyril, Gregory, Bernard and the *Imitation of Christ.*

Here is the final plea of Blésilla to Flaminia in favor of the contemplative life:

> If you have for virtue a passionate love—a simple love is not enough—you must be willing to die for it—then will it bring naught but blessedness and felicity. God inspires the will and the desire of those who love with a great love that exceeds their powers through faith in him and hope in his grace. With courage, then, flee [corruption]. We have our wings. Seek the God of Jacob, the face of God, as Bernard says, the face Jacob saw when he said, "I have seen God face to face, and yet my life is preserved." [3] I tell you this, Flaminia, that you may understand how marvelous is the exchange of this vile, transitory, ephemeral life for life eternal. And you still hold back! You still do not leave the court, the turmoil of the town and the crowd. And you do not say with Paul to those upon the seas of the world, "We are fools in Christ."
>
> Don't think that everything I have said would lead you to live alone. It is not good for a woman to live alone. No! I am suggesting that you withdraw from the throng with a few elect spirits and that you choose certain figures against whom to measure yourself. As Seneca advised Lucilius to take Cato, or if he is too exacting then Laelius, so I would propose Jerome and if he is too exacting, then Augustine.
>
> Retire [like Elijah] for forty days (I mean for your whole life) and having taken food go to Horeb the mount of God. The food is the word of God, which is sovereign, sharper than a two edged sword, penetrating to the division of soul and body. Your soul will be separated from your body and you will then have no struggle to separate yourself from the court and the city, as you do now. Do not wait, I repeat. Blaze with the fire that is never extinguished, never flickers.

I mean the word of God, not the fire of the passions and lust. Shall we not cry with Augustine, "Give thyself to me, my God. Give thyself. See how I love thee and if I love not enough give me the more to love." [4] Shall we not with him love God with a love and élan which are their own reward? We feed on the words of life eternal, ever breaking the bonds of the world. We enter the gardens of the bridegroom and faint for love of him, believing that the sole felicity is to love and be loved by him. O Flaminia, this peace is to be longed for. How important to know how to gain it.! Love is the way, love by which all is brought into existence. By such fervent love we are upheld, love without measure, for here the measure itself is to love without measure, with all the longing of the words of the psalm, "How lovely is thy dwelling place, O Lord of hosts! My soul longs, yea faints for the courts of the Lord." [5]

Flaminia is not persuaded. For her the greater heroism is to be in the world and remain unspotted by the world. The conclusion is that each must be faithful to her own persuasion.

### BIBLIOGRAPHY AND NOTES

This little sketch is based entirely on the article by Leon Bourdion and Odette Sauvage, "Recherches sur Luisa Sigea," *Bulletin des Études Portugaises*, XXXI (1970), pp. 33-176. I am grateful to Elisabeth Hirsch for bringing this article to my attention.

1. Jer. 9:21.
2. Letter 22, pp. 130-33.
3. Gen. 31:31.
4. Conf. XIII, 8-9.
5. Pp. 164-5. Ps. 84:2.

# SCOTLAND

The women deeply involved in the religious movements in Scotland in the age of the Reformation were with one exception intimately connected with John Knox, whether by antipathy or adulation. Unhappily most of our information about them comes to us only from his pen because he wrote so much and what he wrote was preserved. A pivotal figure he was but by no means the initiator of the Reformation in Scotland. When he assumed the helm, the Protestant movement was already so strong that the land was on the verge of civil war.[1] To understand the confrontations we must briefly review the background with the stages in the maturing of Knox's ideas and of his active participation.

The doctrines of the Reformation had infiltrated into Scotland well before the second half of the century. In 1545 Mary of Guise, the Queen Regent, was informed that heresy had so far penetrated that to stem it by punishment was futile. Two years earlier Cardinal Beaton had made the attempt. He was a prince of the church, an astute diplomat, the father of eight illegitimate children, a stalwart champion of the establishment, who instituted a hunt for heretics. Six were condemned to death, among them a woman named Helen Stark (or Stirk). The account of their trials and executions is recorded by John Foxe in his *Acts and Monuments* on the basis of information supplied from Scotland. He was informed that someone had interrupted the sermon

of a friar and another had hung up an image of St. Francis with
a ram's horn on the head and a cow's tail on the rump. As for
the woman here is his account: [2]

The woman Hellen Stirke was accused, for that in her
childbed she was not accustomed to call upon the name of
the Virgin Mary, being exhorted thereto by her neighbours,
but only upon God for Jesus Christ's sake; and because she
said, in like manner, that if she herself had been in the time
of the Virgin Mary, God might have looked to her humility
and base estate, as he did to the Virgin's, in making her the
mother of Christ: thereby meaning, that there were no merits in the Virgin, which procured her that honour, to be
made the mother of Christ, and to be preferred before other
women, but that only God's free mercy exalted her to that
estate: which words were counted most execrable in the face
of the clergy, and of the whole multitude. . . .

After sentence given, their hands were bound, and the
men cruelly treated; which thing the woman beholding, desired likewise to be bound by the sergeants with her husband
for Christ's sake. There was great intercession made by the
town in the mean season for the life of these persons afore-
named, to the governor, who of himself was willing so to
have done, that they might have been delivered: but the
governor was so subject to the appetite of the cruel priests,
that he could not do that which he would.

The woman desired earnestly to die with her husband, but
she was not suffered; yet, following him to the place of exe-
cution, she gave him comfort, exhorting him to perseverance
and patience for Christ's sake, and, parting from him with
a kiss, said on this manner, "Husband, rejoice, for we have
lived together many joyful days; but this day, in which we
must die, ought to be most joyful unto us both because we
must have joy for ever; therefore I will not bid you good
night, for we shall suddenly meet with joy in the kingdom
of heaven." The woman, after that, was taken to a place to
be drowned, and albeit she had a child sucking on her
breast, yet this moved nothing the unmerciful hearts of the

enemies. So, after she had commended her children to the neighbours of the town for God's sake, and the sucking bairn was given to the nurse, she sealed up the truth by her death.

In the year 1546, again at the instigation of Cardinal Beaton, a martyrdom occurred destined to affect the entire course of the Reformation. The Protestant preacher, George Wishart, was burned. He was the mentor of John Knox, who by the death of his master was definitely rescued from the "puddle of Papacy." [3] One year later Beaton was assassinated by certain Protestants with all the solemnity of a religious ritual. The conspirators took refuge in the castle of St. Andrews, where Knox joined himself to them as chaplain. The castle under siege might have resisted successfully save for the arrival of ships from France then in league with Scotland. After surrender, the leaders were treated as prisoners, the lesser sort, including Knox, went to the galleys. He continued at the oars until a treaty between France and England procured his release. For the remainder of the reign of Edward VI he remained in England, at first with pastorates on the northern border, then with a royal chaplaincy in London. The accession of Mary Tudor and the restoration of Catholicism drove him to the continent. He returned briefly by sea to Scotland to marry and bring his bride and mother-in-law to Geneva. Of that more later. He continued then as the leader of the congregation of English exiles in Geneva, until in 1559 the death of Mary and the accession of Elizabeth led to the dispersion of the refugee congregation and Knox's return to Scotland.

He arrived with certain unshakable convictions of which the foremost was that the Mass was idolatry.[4] In a tract on that subject he failed to adduce the most logical argument that the idolatry consists in worshiping bread rather than God. He stressed rather the point that the Mass cannot be a sacrifice because Christ was sacrificed once and for all upon the cross. A further point was that the Mass is not an ordinance of God but rather an invention of man, because so divergent from the original Lord's Supper. In the "papistical mass" the congregation sees "duckings, noddings, crossings, turning and uplifting which all are nothing but a diabolical profanation of Christ's Supper," where all offer thanks, humbly confess themselves redeemed only through Christ's blood and "sit at ane tabill." The withholding of the cup from the laity is another accretion. Knox showed no little erudition in pinpointing the times when each innovation had been introduced. For what reason all this should have been called idolatry is not clear, though Knox said anything in religion invented by the brain of man is idolatry. Whatever the logic, the conviction was plain: the Mass is idolatry and idolatry is worthy of death, whether inflicted by man or by God through plagues and disasters. The role played by heresy for the Catholic was transferred by Knox to idolatry.[5]

The second contention was that women should not exercise rulership. This view Knox set forth in a tract entitled *The First Blast Against the Monstrous Regiment of Women*.[6] Monstrous meant against nature and regiment meant rule. Knox had in mind specifically two women rulers. The first was that "wicked Jezebel," "Bloody Mary," in England from whose persecution he was then in flight in Geneva. The other was the Queen Regent in Scotland, commonly called Mary of Guise, the most Catholic family in France. On the death of her husband, King James V, she had been crowned as regent. Knox said that to put a crown on her head was like "putting a saddle on an unruly cow." [7]

If Knox had confined his invective to these two he would have been on sounder ground, but he launched into a diatribe against women in general as unsuited for governmental office. To elevate a woman to rule is to "defile, pollute and prophane the throne and seat of God." The familiar New Testament texts were, of course, marshalled that women should not have authority over men (1 Tim. 2:12) and should receive instruction from their husbands (1 Cor. 11:3). The Bible is confirmed by nature, which paints women as "frail, impatient, feeble and foolish." Experience shows them to be "inconstant, variable, cruel and lacking the spirit of counsel and regiment." It is against nature that "the foolish, mad and phrenetic should govern the discrete and give counsel to such as be of sober mind." The brute beasts are not so degenerate. "No man ever saw the lion stoop before the lioness." The nobility of England and Scotland, who suffer a woman to rule, are "inferior to brute beasts." The doctors of the church confirm the Bible and nature. Tertullian called woman the "porte and gate of the Devil." The conclusion is that "to promote woman to rule is repugnant to nature, and contumely to God." "This monstriferous empire of women, amongst all the enormities that this day do abound upon the face of the whole earth, is the most detestable and damnable."

Then Knox becomes specific. England, by betraying herself to the proud Spaniard, pandered to the inordinate appetite of that cruel monster Mary and the foolish governors of Scotland, yielding to a crafty dame, have resigned themselves to France. A woman reigning over man should be removed. Those who defend such impiety should be subject to death. Oaths made to such monsters are not binding. Let not that wicked Jezebel of England brag to have overcome Wyatt's rebellion. She has not triumphed over God. We cannot forget Latimer, Ridley and Lady Jane. Mary's reign will speedily cease. "The Trumpet hath once blown."

In the midst of this perfervid vindictiveness Knox introduced one exception: "God by his singular providence and grace exempted Deborah from the common malediction given to women." This left open the possibility that God might do the like again.

A further conviction was that rulers violating God's commands might be forcibly resisted even by the common man. The doctrine of legitimate resistance to rulers, not by passive disobedience but by the sword, had swiftly matured among the Protestants in little over a decade after 1550. The earlier view had been that the only proper course for a Christian was the refusal of obedience. Luther took this position when his translation of the New Testament was suppressed by the emperor, but when that same emperor undertook to stamp out Lutheranism, the citizens of Magdeburg issued a manifesto in 1550 [8] declaring that, although indeed a private citizen might never wield the sword, one magistrate might resist another, the inferior against the superior. In Germany that meant that the electors might depose the emperor whom they had elected. Luther concurred. But this doctrine ceased to be useful for the Lutherans after they had secured toleration by the Peace of Augsburg in 1555. The Calvinists, who

**E bi.     F ij.**

**No Queene in her kingdome can or ought
to syt fast,
If Knokes or Goodmans bookes blowe
any true blast.**

The above is one of a series of satirical cartoons against the Protestants in the tract, *An Oration Against the Vnlawfull Insurrections of the Protestants by Peter Frarin of Antwerp* (Antwerp 1562). The inscription beneath reads:

> No Queene in her kingdome can or ought to syt fast,
> If Knokes or Goodmans bookes blowe any true blast.

Goodman was Christopher Goodman, Knox's associate at Geneva, who published in 1558 the tract *How Superior Powers Ought to Be Obeyed*.

were not included in that peace, took over the idea. For them the inferior magistrates were the princes of the blood who might resist the superior magistrate, in this case the king. Calvin discountenanced the conspiracy of Amboise, led only by a private citizen, but endorsed the armed resistance of the Huguenots in the first war of religion, because they were led by the Prince de Condé of the royal house of Bourbon.

This attempt to be both constitutional and revolutionary broke down under pressure. Calvin's associate Beza already in 1554 was willing to let the private citizen serve as the executor of God's judgment.[9] Such also was the view of Christopher Goodman,[10] a very close friend of Knox at Geneva, who had come to be of similar mind prior to the return to Scotland.[11]

A final conviction was that Catholics cannot be trusted. Do they not teach that the church keeps no faith with one who has no faith? A breach of promise to heretics is in their eyes no perjury.[12] In line with such teaching had not Mary Tudor on her accession promised religious liberty and then kindled the fires of Smithfield? And Mary of Guise had gone back on her promises. Knox called her "crafty and perfidious." He was prepared to believe the same of her daughter, Mary Stuart.

She in the meantime was still in France where she had been queen until the death of her husband, Francis II, in December 1560. Not until a year and a half later did she assume her role as Queen of Scots. Like Knox, she came with some firm convictions. The first was that she was a Catholic and intended so to remain. She made the point very explicit in conversation with the English ambassador. Said she, "I have been brought up in this religion; and who might credit me in anything if I should show myself light in this case?" She had discussed such matters with her uncle, the Cardinal of Lorraine and found "no great reason to change my opinion." The ambassador hoped for "a unity of religion in all Christendom." She agreed, "but for my part, you may perceive I am none of those that will change my religion every year." [13]

The other point was her determination to be the ruler and no symbolic queen of Scotland. Well before her return she had heard reports of the unruliness of her subjects. The English ambassador reported to Queen Elizabeth a statement made to him by Mary (Nov. 17, 1560) [14]

> My subjects in Scotland (quoth she), do their duty in nothing, nor have they performed their part in one thing that belongeth to them. I am their Queen, and so they call me, but they use me not so; they have done what pleaseth them. . . . I will have them assemble by my authority, and proceed in their doings by the laws of the realm, which they so much boast of and keep none of them. . . . I am their Sovereign, but they take me not so; they must be taught to know their duties.

She was referring to the events which had lately transpired. Her mother had sought to restrain the Protestants. In answer to her summons they had arrived in steel bonnets and even went so far as to depose her in October 1559. She died in less than a year thereafter (June 10, 1560). The estates proceeded to draft the Treaty of Edinburgh (1560), which included the provision that in Scotland the jurisdiction of the pope was to be abolished and the Mass interdicted on pain of confiscation of goods for the first offense, exile for the second and death for the third.

Mary arrived on the 19th of August, 1561, bringing with her, according to Knox, "Sorrow, dolour, darkness and all impiety." [15] She was at once called upon to ratify the treaty and at once objected to the interdiction of the Mass. To the English ambassador she explained: [16]

> You know (quoth she), there is much ado in my realm about matters of religion; and though there be a greater number of a contrary religion unto me than I would there were, yet there is no reason that subjects should give a law to their Sovereign, and specially in matters of religion, which, I fear (quoth she), my subjects shall take in hand.

The ambassador answered:

> Religion is of the greatest force that may be. You have been long out of your realm, so as the contrary religion to yours has won the upper hand, and the greatest part of your realm. Your mother was a woman of great experience, of deep dis-

simulation, and kept that realm in quietness, till she began to constrain men's consciences; and as you think it unmeet to be constrained by your subjects, so it may like you to consider the matter is also intolerable to them to be constrained by you in matters of conscience; for the duty due to God cannot be given to any other without offence of his Majesty.

Why (said she), God does command subjects to be obedient to their Princes, and commands Princes to read his law, and govern thereby themselves and the people committed to their charges.

Yea, Madam (quoth I), in those things that be not against his commandments.

Well (quoth she), I will be plain with you; the Religion that I profess, I take to be most acceptable to God: and, indeed, neither do I know nor desire to know any other. Constancy does become all folks well, but none better than princes, and such as have rule over realms, and especially in matters of Religion. . . . I mean to constrain none of my subjects; and I trust they should have no support to constrain me.

Mary then proceeded to have Mass celebrated in her private chapel in defiance of the interdiction of parliament. The moderates were inclined to let her have her way, provided she kept her word not to constrain her subjects. Even Knox might have been willing to let her go to perdition in her own way had he trusted her. Mary Tudor had made a like promise and the end was the fires of Smithfield.

There are modern interpreters who insist that Mary of Scots was not another Mary of England, but rather a liberal Catholic reared in France in an atmosphere of latitudinarianism.[17] Her mentor in younger years had been her uncle, the Cardinal of Lorraine, himself suspected of Lutheranism because he was willing to enter into dialogue with Lutherans and even Calvinists. True, but his object was simply to refute them. Rumor had it that he was so indifferent to religion as to advise Mary to turn Anglican to insure her accession to the throne of England.[18] He might indeed have counseled dissimulation in order to gain the power to suppress Anglicanism. At any rate he showed no mercy, when, after the collapse of the conspiracy of Amboise, he visited hideous reprisals upon the defeated. He was a *politique* like the later Richelieu, who suppressed Protestants at home while abetting Protestants abroad.

Mary's second mentor in France was Catherine de Medici, who took Mary under her wing when she became the queen of her son Francis II. Catherine, too, was a *politique*, who initiated the Colloquy of Poissy in the hope of reconciling the parties and insuring peace in the land, but when it did not come, instigated the massacre of St. Bartholomew. Mary would not have imbibed in France a Catholicism without fangs.

Knox was the more convinced she was no tolerant liberal when her first "private" Mass was anything but private. We have a description from the pen of a Scot writing to Elizabeth's Lord Secretary. Said he: [19]

> What troubles have arisen in this country for religion your Honour knoweth. All things are now grown into such a liberty, and her Grace taketh unto herself such a will to do therein what she lists, that of late, contrary to her own ordinances, as great numbers have repaired to her chapel to hear mass, as sometimes come to a common church to hear sermon. To have her mind alter'd for this freedom she desireth to have all men live as they list: she can hardly be brought, and thinketh it too great a subjection for her being a prince in her own country, to have her will broken therein. The subjects that desire to live in the true worship and fear of God offer rather their lives again to be sacrificed, than that they would suffer again such an abomination, yea, almost permit herself to enjoy the mass, which is now more plainly and openly spoken against by the preachers than ever was the Pope of Rome. This kindleth in her a desire to revenge, and breedeth in others a liberty to speak, and a will to attempt to mend that by force which by no other means they can get reformed.

The writer adds that in connection with her Mass two blasphemies occurred. A schoolmaster, to affront the ministers, baptized a cat in the name of the Father, the Son and the Holy

Ghost. The queen's singing master asserted that he would give no more credit to the New Testament than to a tale of Robin Hood except it were confirmed by the doctors of the church. Knox said that the queen, when she went on tour, took her Mass with her and "all parts she polluted with her idolatry." [20]

Knox in a sermon blazed. That one Mass, said he, "was more fearful to him than if ten thousand armed enemies were landed in any part of the realm of purpose to suppress the whole religion." [21] Mary summoned him to her presence and "had long reasoning with him." [22]

Then ensued the famous confrontations [23] in which Knox has often been portrayed as a blustering bigot badgering a simple lass. But Knox this time did not bluster and Mary was by no means simple. She accused him at first of having raised up a part of her subjects against her mother and herself. He replied that he had never stirred up sedition. In fact, he had discountenanced the rampant image breaking of the "rascal multitude." But, continued Mary, he had written a book against the regiment of women. Yes, he had, but it was not meant for her but rather for that Jezebel in England. This was disingenuous, for although there was no attack on Mary of Scots there was against her mother. Knox went on to say that so long as she did not defile her hands with the blood of the saints he would be content to live under her "Grace as Paul was to live under Nero." Knox had a genius for the infelicitous. What he meant, of course, was that Paul had enjoined obedience to rulers and the ruler in his day happened to be Nero.

She pressed him. If God commands subjects to obey their princes how can you teach people "to receive another religion than that which their princes can allow?"

"Because," Knox explained, "right religion does not stem from the authority of princes but from the eternal God." Abraham did not submit to the religion of Pharaoh, the apostles to that of the Roman emperors or David to that of Nebuchadnezzar.

"Yes," she answered, "but none of these men raised the sword against their princes."

"God, Madam, had not given unto them the power and the means. Think ye that subjects having power may resist their princes? If their princes exceed their bounds . . . they may be resisted even by power," just as an insane father may be restrained from killing his children. If princes would murder the children of God, they may be bound and imprisoned. This is "no disobedience . . . because it agreeth with the will of God."

At this Mary was so taken aback that for a quarter of an hour she stood amazed. Then, recovering composure, she told him that what he was saying added up to this that her subjects should obey him rather than her and she would be subject to them rather than they to her.

Knox answered that both subjects and princes must obey God who "craves of kings that they be as it were foster-fathers to the Church."

"Yea (said she), but ye are not the Kirk I will nourish. I will defend the Kirk of Rome, for it is, I think, the true Kirk of God."

Knox said "her thought did not make that Roman harlot to be the true and immaculate spouse of Jesus Christ."

"My conscience (said she) is not so."

"Conscience, Madam (said he), requires knowledge and I fear that right knowledge ye have none." He had in mind the etymology of the word *conscientia* from *con* and *scientia,* with knowledge. Since Mary was not properly informed, she could have no conscience. She said she had read. "So (said he) did the Jews that crucified Christ read both the Law and the Prophets." Reading is not enough. One must correctly understand.

Here Mary caught his heel. "Ye interpret the Scriptures in one manner and they (the Catholics) in another. Whom shall I believe?"

The problem became acute for Protestants when their own divergencies defied resolution. Knox had not yet sensed the problem. "The Word of God," said he, "is plain in the self and if there appears any obscurity in one place, the Holy Ghost explains the same more clearly in other places." The Mass is obviously an invention of man because Jesus did not order Mass to be said at his Last Supper.

"Ye are oure sair (too hard) for me (said the Queen), but if they were here that I have heard they would answer you."

"Would to God that the learnedest Papist in Europe were

present . . . for then ye should hear the vanity of the Papistical religion." They cannot "sustain an argument except by fire and sword . . . They won't come to a conference, unless that themselves were admitted for judges."

At this point the disputants adjourned for dinner, Knox hoping that the commonwealth of Scotland would be as blessed under Mary as the commonwealth of Israel under Deborah—that blessed exception in the *First Blast*.

A second encounter had to do with Mary's marriage. She was a lovely eligible widow. She was also a queen, and royal marriages entailed political alliances. To be perfectly free as to marriage a queen would have to abdicate. Knox feared that if Mary married again a Frenchman or a Spaniard, as Mary Tudor had done, Catholicism would be restored in Scotland. The husband of Mary of Scots must be a Protestant and preferably a Scot or an Englishman, for Knox desired the union of the two kingdoms. He gave public voice to his view. Mary called him in.

"What have ye to do," she demanded, "with my marriage? Or what are ye within this Commonwealth?"

"A subject born within the same, Madam," said he, "and albeit I be neither Earl, Lord, nor Baron within it, yet has God made me (how abject I be in your eyes) a profitable member within the same. Yet, Madam, to me it appertains no less to forewarn of such things as may hurt it, if I foresee them, than it does to any of the Nobility, for both my vocation and conscience crave plainness of me." This was a proclamation of the divine right of the commoner against the divine right of the crown and more than that, it was the divine right of the prophet to instruct the sovereign.

Mary wept. Knox assured her that he could scarcely "abide the tears of my own boys whom my own hand corrects, much less can I rejoice in your Majesty's weeping, but I must sustain (albeit unwillingly) your Majesty's tears rather than I dare hurt my conscience or betray my Commonwealth through my silence."

Mary need not detain us longer. She continued, of course, to play the pivotal role in the plot of the Catholic extremists to remove Elizabeth by assassination from the throne of England that Mary, as her successor, might restore Catholicism. But the crux of Mary's personal confrontation with Protestantism is already abundantly evident in the encounter with Knox. The rift between them epitomizes the clashing of ideologies in an age of dying and killing for religion.

## NOTES

1. "The Scotish Correspondence of Mary of Lorraine," *Publications of the Scotish Historical Society,* Third Ser. vol. X, (1927), p. xi.
2. John Foxe, *Acts and Monuments* V (1838), pp. 624-5.
3. *History of the Reformation in Scotland,* ed. William Croft Dickinson, 2 vols. (1849), 1, p. xxxxii.
4. *A Vindication of the Doctrine that the Sacrifice of the Mass Is Idolatry* (1550) *Works,* ed. David Laing, 6 vol. (Edinburgh, 1846-8), III, pp. 29-70.
5. *Works* IV, p. 398, III, pp. 67-68 and *Hist.* II, pp. 122-3.
6. *Works* IV, pp. 364-420. The passages cited are from pages in this order: 397, 379, 373, 393, 396, 382, 373, 368, 411, 415, 416, 418-9, 405.
7. *Hist.* I, p. 116.
8. Knox cites this document *Hist.* II, pp. 129-30.
9. Robert Kingdon, *Bibl.d'Hum. et Renaissance* XXII (1960), pp. 566-9.
10. Christopher Goodman, *How Superior Powers Ought to Be Obeyed,* Facsimile Text Soc. (1931).
11. A good review by William Croft Dickinson in his introduction to Knox's *History,* pp. xl-xlii.
12. *Hist.* I, p. 180.
13. *Ibid.,* I, p. 366.
14. Great Britain Public Record Office, *Calendar of State Papers Foreign,* III, pp. 1560-61. Throcmorton to Elizabeth.
15. *Hist.* II, p. 7.
16. *Ibid.,* I, pp. 367-8.
17. For example Antonia Fraser, *Mary Queen of Scots* (New York, 1969).
18. Great Britain Public Record Office, *Calendar of State Papers relating to Scotland* vol. I (1898), No. 1077, p. 603.
19. Robert Keith, *History of the Affairs of Church and State in Scotland* II (1845), pp. 268-9. Observe note I.
20. *Hist.* II, p. 20.
21. *Ibid.,* II, p. 12
22. *Ibid.,* II, 13.
23. *Ibid.,* pp. 12-22 and 82-84.

# Elizabeth and
# Marjory Bowes

Knox's tenderness in ministering to the spiritual ailments of women offers a striking contrast to his bluntness in the confrontations with the Queen. The great difference, of course, is that the troubled souls were on the Lord's side. Even so, one is amazed to find expressions of respect for women from the pen of one who had stigmatized them as "frail, impatient, feeble, foolish, inconstant, variable, cruel and phrenetic." How could he possibly go so far then as to say that they ministered to him as much as he to them? The anomoly attracted the attention of Robert Louis Stevenson who made this discerning comment:

The sexes, irrespective of marriage, will know not love only, but all those other ways in which man and woman naturally make each other happy—by sympathy, by admiration, by the atmosphere they bear about them. . . . For, through all this gradation, the difference of sex makes itself pleasurably felt. Down to the most lukewarm courtesies of life, there is a special chivalry due and a special pleasure received, when the two sexes are brought ever so lightly into contact. We love our mothers otherwise than we love our fathers; a sister is not as a brother to us; and friendship between man and woman, be it never so unalloyed and innocent, is not the same as friendship between man and man. Knox was capable of those intimacies with women that em-

bellished his life; a man ever ready to comfort weeping
women, and to weep along with them. . . . The *ewigweibliche*
(eternal feminine) was as necessary to him as to Goethe. . . .
He made himself necessary to troubled hearts and minds . . .
and those whom he had thus helped became dear to him,
and were made the constant companions of his leisure if they
were at hand, or encouraged and comforted by letter if they
were afar.[1]

One of the most intimate feminine friendships of Knox was
with Elizabeth Bowes, a religious melancholic who craved spiritual ministrations as frequently as a diabetic requires injections.
After her death he described their relationship in these words: [2]

I would declare unto the world what was the cause of our
great familiarity and long acquaintance. . . . I have heard
the complaints of divers that fear God, but of the like conflict which she sustained, from the time of our first acquaintance until this hour, I have not known. For her temptation
was not in the flesh but in the spirit, for Satan did continually buffet her by reason of her former idolatry and other
iniquities: for the which I have seen her pour forth tears
oft'er than ever I heard man or woman in my life. Her company to me was comfortable but it was not without some
cross, for my mind was seldom quiet for doing something for
her troubled conscience.

Knox assured her that ministering to her distress was no
burden.[3] "Think not, Sister, that I esteem it any trouble to
comfort you. No other labor, save only blowing my Master's
trumpet shall impede me to do the uttermost in my power." He
laments that they cannot "remane togidder for mutuall comfort."
If she needs him, he also needs her, because he sees in her anxie-
ties "the verie mirrour and glass wharin I behold myself."
"Though I am forced to thunder out the threatenings of God
against obstinate rebels, yet I am worse than my pen can express.
I am no adulterer but the heart is infected with foul lusts. I am
no idolator but the heart loveth the self. I am no man killer, but
I help not my needy brother." The subtle serpent had poured

into him the venom of pride by reason of the flattery of his preaching. Elizabeth Bowes had brought him solace. "Your letters were onto my heart some comfort, for I find a congruance between us in spirit, being so far distant in body." "Your infirmity has been unto me occasion to search the Scripture more ne'er than ever I could do in my own cause."

Yet for all the comfort the relationship was not easy. She was the wife of Sir Robert Bowes to whom she had borne fifteen children. He was not of her religious persuasion and was very upset when their daughter Marjory was married to John Knox.[4] Some have suspected Mrs. Bowes of engineering the match in order without scandal to have greater access to the son-in-law. But there is no indication that either Knox or Marjory was constrained. He was attracted to the daughter and she was attractive. Calvin called her *suavissima* "highly engaging" and after her death consoled Knox that her like was not readily to be found.[5] He testified to his affection when he told the mother there was none with whom he would rather speak than with "the one whom God had offered him and commanded him to love as his own flesh." Still the only extant letter to Marjory is not a perfumed note. It had to do with how best to handle her mother's "troubled conscience" and concluded, "I think this be the first letter that I ever wrote you." [6]

Knox first met the mother and daughter while in England.[7] With the commencement of Mary Tudor's persecution he fled unmarried to the continent. Then came back, married and took bride and mother with him to Geneva. On the accession of Elizabeth, the Knoxes removed to Scotland. Elizabeth Bowes did not join her irate husband, but planted herself on the wedded couple. No doubt she would be useful caring for the two little boys Marjory had borne in Geneva and Marjory could take more time to serve as Knox's amanuensis, a task at which she was often so tired she could not remember what she had written the day before. Living with a hypochondriac mother, who monopolized her husband's attention, must have been a cross. After his wife's death Knox married Margaret Stuart, of royal blood, she seventeen, he around fifty. She presented him with three daughters. When this was reported to King James, he exclaimed, "God be thanked, for an they had been three lads, I had never bruiked my three kingdoms in peace."

But to return to the correspondence with Mrs. Bowes.[8] Her spiritual troubles were twofold: that her sins in the past were too heinous to be forgiven and that she might sin again in the future. She wrote to Knox, "Alas, wretched woman that I am, for the self-same sins that reigned in Sodom and Gomorrah reign in me."

"Oh, come now," replied Knox in effect, "the sins of those cities were violence against strangers and unnatural filthiness. Of which of these are you guilty? Do you think that every stirring and motion of the flesh, the very ardent and burning lust, is the sin of Sodom? God forbid that you should think so."

Then she was fearful that with the restoration of Catholicism in England she might be guilty of "abominable and blasphemous idolatry" by doing reverence to the Host. Knox replied, "I am sure that your heart neither thirsts nor desires to invoke or make prayer to bread. Alas Sister, your imbecility troubles me that I should know you so weak that you should be moved for so small a matter. But your weakness is not reckoned, but by Jesus our Lord is excused, 'For he breaks not down the bruised reed, nor yet quencheth forth the smoking flax,' which words are to us most comfortable."

Knox consoled her that her experience was not unique. "There is no temptation that has yet apprehended you which does not commonly assault the elect of God. The soul of the very elect is always flowing and troubled with some fear. Some time God does turn away his face apparently even from his elect and then are they in anguish and care. Jesus himself was tempted to idolatry. Satan, this roaring lion, when repulsed, departed only for a time."

Suffering in the spirit is profitable. God allows his children to be tried as by fire and hides his face from them that "his presence after may be delectable. Further, Sister, such as tastes the cup of desperation without any motion or thirst of grace never tastes any sweetness of God's promises. I know that your cup to be most bitter, but profitable. These dolors and infirmities be most profitable for us, for by the same is our pride beaten down." The angel touched the marrow of Jacob's thigh, whereby he became "crooked and unable to wrestle." Only after that did the angel give his blessing. Whereby we see "it is necessary that our thighs be touched and we made crooked, that is, that all help and comfort of the flesh be taken from us, that we may learn to depend on the promises of our most faithful God."

"Your very distress shows that you are in God's favor . . . Your sorrow for guilt proves the knowledge of God's goodness . . . If you hate Jesus you would not be seeking my company . . . The sheep are those who crave the shepherd's voice. Your lament over the temptation to idolatry shows that you hate it. Be not troubled that only a few are chosen. You are of the small 'contemnit' flock to whom the Father gives his kingdom."

"Despair not of God's mercy. The Scripture in sundry places attributes to God mutable passions that are not in God, as that he repented of having made Saul king, or that he plagues the world in his anger, and yet no such thing can be in the Godhead. Then would ye inquire, 'How shall we be assured of God's favor which changeth not?' 'By his word.' Truly neither thought nor deed shall be imputed onto you, for they are remitted in Christ's blood. Did not God proclaim his own name in the ears of Moses, saying, 'I the Lord, merciful, benign, forgiving sin, transgression and iniquity'? I do confess my right ear, my right thumb, my right toe must be sprinkled with the blood of the Lamb."

"Jesus Christ is all sufficient for us . . . Therefore abide patiently the Lord's deliverance to the end, remembering that our Head is entered into his kingdom by troubles and dolors without number. Most lamentably he complained in these words, 'My God! my God! why hast thou forsaken me?' He did not only suffer poverty, hunger, blasphemy and death, but also he did taste the cup of God's wrath against sin, not only to make full satisfaction for his chosen people, but also that he might learn to be pitiful to such as are tempted."

"For you, Sister, I only lament your corporal trouble, which albeit it be painful yet is it transitory and shortly shall have an end, the dolor thereof recompensed above all that man's heart can ask or devise. For the afflictions of this life are not worthy of that glory which shall be shown forth in us, whom God our Father hath appointed to be like the image of his only Son, Jesus

Christ. . . . Seeing then that we have a Bishop that by experience has learned in himself to have compassion upon our dolors and infirmities, we ought with good reason to quiet ourselves, undoubtedly knowing that he who has vanquished in himself has vanquished for us . . . And so, if flesh would suffer greatly ought we to rejoice that it hath pleased the goodness of our God to print in our hearts the seal of his mercy."

## NOTE

1. Robert Louis Stevenson, "John Knox and his Relations with Women," *Familiar Studies in Men and Books* (London, 1924), pp. 224-5.
2. *Works* VI, p. 514.
3. The letters are in *Works III*, pp. 331-402; IV, pp. 217-8; VI, pp. 515-20. The quotations following are from III, 368, 337-9, 387, 338-9, 379.
4. *History* I, p. lxxxiii, note 4.
5. *Calvini Opera* XVIII, No. 3340, p. 365; No. 3377, p. 435, No. 3378.
6. On Knox's affection for Marjory, *Works* III, pp. 369, 379. His letter to her *Ibid.* p. 370 The father's displeasure p. 376.
7. Biographical details in D. P. Thomson, *Women of the Scotish Reformation* (1960), including the ejaculation of King James on p. 19.
8. The following quotations are from *Works* III, pp. 344, 361, 367 346, 356, 368, 339, 349, 381, 340, 399, 373, 349, 390, 371, 351, 363, 365, 381, 391, 377, 359.

# Anne Locke

Anne Locke, in the judgment of Robert Louis Stevenson, was the woman Knox loved most. Who can tell? Certainly in his relationship with her there was no touch of the cross, no need to solace incessant bemoanings. To Anne Locke he could write that he needed a horse. Anne was the daughter of a merchant adventurer, who did his best to save William Tyndale. She was married to Henry Locke, another merchant of cultivated tastes and Protestant leanings, without that passionate commitment which he respected but did not share with his wife. Knox met Anne in London on his way to Geneva. When the persecution under Mary Tudor became acute he besought Mrs. Locke to leave her husband and join him in Geneva. A personal interest was avowed. "Ye writ that your desyre is ernist to sie me, Deir Sister, yf I shuld expres the thirst and langoure whilk I haif for your presence, I would appear to pass measure." Let her take refuge in Geneva that "maist perfyt schoole of Chryst that ever was in the erth since the dayis of the Apostillis."

Henry Locke was not at all happy over her departure with two of the children, but her leaving did not disrupt the marriage. Quite possibly she had to leave England because of her outspoken Protestantism, whereas he, by reason of lukewarmness, might remain. On the accession of Elizabeth, Anne returned and joined him. A copy in the British Museum of her work written in Geneva bears the inscription *Liber Henrici Lock ex dono Annae uxoris suae 1559.*

# SERMONS

# OF JOHN CAL-
## VIN, VPON THE SONGE
### that Ezechias made af-
ter he had bene ficke, and
afflicted by the hand of
God,
conteyned in the 38.Chapi-
ter of Efay.

¶ Tranflated out of Frenche
into Englifhe.
1560.

# TO THE RIGHT
## HONORABLE, AND
*Chriftian Princeffe,the Lady*
*Katharine,Ducheffe*
*of Suffolke.*

*Concernyng my tranflation of this boke, it*
*may pleafe you to vnderftand that I haue rē-*
*dred it fo nere as I poffibly might, to the very*
*wordes of his text,and that in fo plaine Eng-*
*lifhe as I could expreffe:  Suche as it is,*
*I befeche your grace to take it*
*good parte.*

Your graces humble
A.  L.

---

Portions of the Title Page, Dedication and Conclusion of Anne Locke's
Translation of Calvin

Knox's departure from Geneva was prior to hers, and on the way to Scotland he wrote her from Dieppe, "As touching remembrance of yow, it cannot be, I say, the corporal absence of one year or two that can quenche in my hart that familiar acquaintance in Christ Jesus, which half a yeare did engender, and almost two yeares did nourish and confirm." When he was back in Scotland and she in London, his letters supply many details about the progress of the Reformation beyond the border.

After the death of Henry Locke in 1571, she was married to Edward Dering, such an able and daring Puritan that he was in trouble with Archbishop Parker and Bishop Sandys by whom he was silenced. Dering died a consumptive in 1576 at the age of thirty-six. Anne's third husband was Richard Prowse, a merchant and a firm Protestant. Of Anne's published works the first bears the initials A. L., the second A. P., for her first and third husbands.

These writings of hers are of especial interest in a work on the role of women, much more so than Knox's letters to her from Edinburgh all about the blowing of the trumpets of Joshua, though these do disclose his need for her spiritual support. In a dire moment he confessed himself "in verie deid in need of her comfort." Would that we had her reply! But we do have two of her translations from the French with prefaces of her own composition.

The first was a rendering of a sermon of John Calvin on King Hezekiah's song of thanksgiving after recovery from an illness. The dedication is to the "Right Honorable, and Christian Princesse, the Lady Katherine, Duchesse of Suffolke." Anne begins with the observation that many persons suffering great soreness of body do show forth great "constancie" of spirit, whereas many who have health and wealth in "suffisance" are assailed in "soule," whereby we see that physicians are needed for more than the body. "He that cureth the sicke minde . . . cureth or preserveth not onely minde but bodye also." For spiritual ailments God, the heavenly physician, has given a "receipe" which "the most excellent Apothecaire master John Calvin hath compounded, and I your Grace's most bounden and humble have put into an English [pill] box, and do present unto you. My thankes are taken away and drowned by the greate excesse of duetie that I owe you. Such remedye as here is contained can no Philosopher, no Infidele, no Papist minister. For what perfite helpe can they geve to a dyseased mynde, that vnderstande not, or beleue not the onely thyng that must of nedefull necessitie be put into all medicines that maye serue for a tormented soule, that is to say, the determined prouidence of almyghtie God, whiche ordreth and disposeth all thynges to the best to them that truste in him?"

To one who "seeth no signe of Gods grace in his soule, but the depe woundes that Gods anger hath left in his conscience, perceiueth no tokeen to argue him th' elect of God. . . . what helpe remaineth in this extremititie? If we thinke the helpe of the Papistes, to begge and borrowe others Virgins oyle that have none to spare, to bye the superfluous workes of those men that say they haue done more than suffiseth to satisfie Gods lawe and to deserue theyr owne saluation. . . . If (I say) we thinks these good & sufficient medicines: we but promise health, & performe death." . . . But the Christian "beyng strong with the stinge of the scorpion knoweth howe with oyle of the same scorpion to be healed agayne: beying wounded with the iustice of God that hateth sinne, he knoweth howe with the mercy of the same God that pardoneth sinne to haue hys peine asswaged and hurt amended."

"So here this good soules Physician hath brought you where you maye se lyinge before youre face the good king Ezechias, somtime chillinge and chattering with colde, somtime languishing & meltyng away with heate, nowe fresing, now frying, nowe spechelesse, now crying out, with other suche piteous panges & passions wrought in his tender afflicted spirit, by giltie conscience of his owne fault, by terrible consideration of Gods iustice, by cruell assaultes of the tyrannous enemie of many saluation, vexynge hym in much more lamentable wise than any bodyly feuer can worke, or bodyly fleshe can suffer. On th' other side for his helpe, you se him sometyme throwe vp his gastly eyen [ghostly eyes], starynge wyth horrour, and scant discernynge for peine and for want of the lyuely moisture to fede the brightnes of theyr sight. You se him sometyme yeldyngly stretch oute, sometyme struglinglye throwe his weakned legges not able to sustein his feble body: sometime he casteth abrode, or holdeth vp his white & blodles hand toward the place whether his soule longeth: sometyme with fallyng chappes, he breatheth out vnperfect soundes, gasping rather than calling for mercy & helpe. These thinges being here laid open to sight. . . . if we feele oure selues in like anguisshe we finde that the disease is the same that Ezechias had, and so by conuenience of reason must by the same meane be healed."

Her second translation was entitled *The Markes of the Children of God* from the French of J. Taffin, a pastor in the Netherlands whose encouragements to his flock she thought would be helpful to sufferers in England in 1590 when Whitgift was endeavoring to suppress the Puritan movement. The tract was dedicated to a fellow woman reformer, the "Right Honorable and vertuous Laide, the Countesse of Warwicke." The preface is of interest in part for the side glimpse of the feeling of a woman as to the restrictions on her sex. She wrote, "But because great things by reason of my sexe, I may not doe, and that which I may, I ought to doe, I haue according to my duetie, brought my poore basket of stones to the strengthening of the wals of that Ierusalem, whereof (by Grace) we are all both Citizens and members."

Her little basket was a Puritan paean of optimism on the glory about to be revealed.

"For what are all the pleasant things of this world, which most bewitch the mindes of men, if they be compared with heauenly and eternall things? If stately & sumptuous buildings do delight; what building is so statelie and glorious as new *Ierusalem?* If riches, what so rich as that, whose pauement is of pure Gold, whose foundations and wals of precious stones, & gates of orient pearls? If Friends, Kinsfolke and neighbours? what Cittie so replenished as this, where God himselfe in his Maiestie, Iesus Christ the head of the Church in his Glory, & all the holy Angels, Patriarkes, Prophets, Apostles & Martirs do dwell together in happinesse for euer? If honour? what honour comparable to this,

to be the seruant and child of so mightie a King, and Heire of
so glorious a Kingdome; where neyther time dooth consume, nor
enuie depriue of honour, nor power of Aduersary spoyle of
Glory, that is endles & incomprehensible? If then there bee no
comparison betweene things Heauenly, and things that are
Earthlie, and no man can attaine to the things that are Heauenly,
but by the same way that Christ himselfe attained vnto them,
which was by the Crosse: why (casting off all impediments that
presseth downe) doe wee not runne on our course with cheerful-
nesse and Hope, hauing Christ so mighty a King, for our Cap-
taine & Guide, who (as the Apostle saith) for the Glory that was
set before him, endured the Crosse, and despising the shame,
sitteth now at the right hand of the Throne of God?"

## BIBLIOGRAPHY

The letters of Knox to Anne Locke are in works VI, pp. 11-15; 20-27,
77-79, 103-104, 107-108 and IV, pp. 237-41. In the same volume there
are his letters to the sisters in Edinburgh. They add but little. Her translation of *Sermons: John Calvin upon the Songe that Ezechias made,*
1560 is signed A. L. for Anne Locke. In the Short Title Catalog no.
4450.
The translation of John Taffin, *The Markes of the Children of God*
(1609) is signed A. P., because her third husband was Richard Prowse.
This is Short Title Catalog no. 23652.
Her second husband was Edward Dering whom we shall shortly meet
in another sketch. Henry Locke died in 1571, Dering in 1576.
There is an admirable treatment of Anne Locke by Patrick Collinson,
"The Role of Women in the English Reformation illustrated by the
Life and Friendships of Anne Locke," *Studies in Church History,* II
(1965).

# ENGLAND REVISITED

# *Katherine Stubbes*

Volume Two in this series included sketches of women in England. I had not intended to add any more until I came across several of especial interest. Katherine Stubbes is the first woman I have found with a genuine interest in theology in the more technical sense, though we can't be quite sure whether the interest was hers or her husband's. We have the account only from his pen. He was a Puritan pamphleteer in the years 1581-93. In 1586 he was married to Katherine Emmes, then only fifteen. His age we do not know. When just over twenty, she gave birth to a "manchild" and within a fortnight could "go abroad in the house." A "quotidian ague" then struck her in which "she languished for the space of sixe weekes or thereabouts" until the end.

The following year her husband published an account of her life and faith. He craved to be believed that she was a "mirroure of womanhood, the rarest Paragon in the world, gentle and courteous of nature, she was never heard to give any the lie, nor to *thou* any in anger. [*Thou* in that day was like *du* in German, *tu* in French, insulting to superiors.] She was never known to fall out with any of her neighbours, nor with the least child that lived; much less to scold or brawl. She was marked above all for the fervent zeal with which she confounded Papists or Atheists to whom she would not yeeld a iot and would most mightily iustifie the truth of God against their blasphemous untruths."

"She obeyed the commandment of the Apostle, who biddeth women to be silent and to learn of their husbands at home.

# A CHRISTALL

## Glasse for Christian Women.

Containing a most excellent Discourse,
of the Godly Life and Christian death of Mistresse
KATHERINE STVBBES, who departed this
Life in Burton vpon Trent in Stafford-
shire, the 14. of December.

With a most heauenly Confession of the Christian Faith, which Shee made a little before her departure,
as also a most wonderfull combate betwixt Satan and her
soule: worthy to be Imprinted in letters
of Gold, and to be ingrauen in
the Table of euery Chri-
stian heart.

Set downe word for word as Shee spake, as neere
as could be gathered: By PHILIP
STVBBES Gent.

REVEL. 14. verse 13.

*Blessed are the dead that die in the Lord, euen so saith the Spirit, for
they rest from their labours, and their workes follow them.*

LONDON

Printed for EDVVARD WHITE, and are to be sold at his
Shoppe neere the little North doore of S. Pauls Church
at the Signe of the Gunne.
1608.

When she was not reading, she would spend the time in con-
ferring, talking and reasoning with her husband of the word of
God, and of Religion: asking him, what is the sense of this
place? And what is the sense of that? How expound you this
place? (Note that she does not use the less respectful thou to her
husband.) So she seemed to be, as it were, ravished with the same
spirit that David was when he said, 'The zeale of thine house
hath eaten me up.' "

She had had well in advance a premonition of death, and now
to the friends gathered about her bed she said, "For that my
houre-glasse is runne out, and that the time for my departure
hence is at hand, I am persuaded to make a profession of my
faith before you all." Her husband declared on the title page of
his *Christall Glasse for Christian Women* that he had "Set downe
word for word as Shee spake, as neere as could be gathered." One
marvels if it be true that a woman dying of quartan fever could
dictate so concise, so complete and so orderly a compendium of
the reformed faith. She treats of the main articles of the Protestant creeds: God, the Trinity, Christ, the forgiveness of sins and
the life to come; salvation by faith alone and predestination,
with the usual defence of the righteousness of God in damning
some and saving others seeing that all deserve damnation. Some
receive it to illustrate his justice. Some are saved to illustrate his
mercy. There is nothing novel in her confession, save perchance
the tone of fervent piety.

Take for example her statement about God.

> I will define him unto you as the spirit of God shall illumi-
> nate my heart. I believe therefore with my hearte, and freely
> confesse with my mouth heere before you all, that this God
> in whom I beleeve, is a most glorious spirit, or spirituall
> substance, a divine essence or essential beinge, without be-
> ginning or ending; of infinite glory, power, might and majes-
> tie: invisible, inaccessible, incomprehensible, and altogether
> unspeakable. I beleeve and confesse, that this glorious God-
> head, this blessed substance, essence or being; that this divine
> power, which we call God, is divided into a Trinity of per-
> sons, the Father, the Sonne and the holy Spirit.

That, being a woman, she should be a theologian is worthy of mark. Her theology is impressive chiefly by majesty of diction and fervor of spirit. More impressive is her welcoming of death that she might penetrate the veil of inaccessibility and behold the light of God's countenance.

And so desirous was she to bee with the Lord, that these golden sentences were never out of her mouth:

"I desire to be dissolved and to be with Christ";

"O miserable wretch that I am, who shall deliver me from this bodie subject to sinne?"

"Come, quickly Lord Jesus, come quickly";

"Like as the hart desireth the water springs, so doth my soul thirst after thee, O God."

"I would rather be a dore keeper in the house of my God, then to dwell in the tents of the wicked," with many other heavenly sentences, which least (lest) I should seeme tedious, I willingly omit. She would alwaies pray in her sickness absolutely that God would take her out of this miserable world. And when her husband and others, would desire her to pray for health, if it were the will of God, she would answere, "I beseech you pray not that I should live, for I think it long to be with my God. Christ is to me life, and death is to me advantage. Yea, the day of death is the day of everlasting life, and I cannot enter into life but by death. Therefore is death the doore or entrance into everlasting life to me. O my God, why not now? why not now? why not now? O my good God, I am ready for thee. I am prepared. O receive me now for thy Christ's sake. O send thy messenger of death to fetch me. Send thy Sergeant to arrest me, thy Pursevant to attach me, thy Herauld to summon me. O send thy Jailer to deliver my soule out of prison.

How like is all of this to the desire of Teresa as a child to flee to the Moors that she might be killed and enjoy at once the vision of God! Teresa pitied the poor Protestants consigned to perdition. Katherine the poor Papists with their blasphemous untruths. And yet both were consumed with the love of God.

## BIBLIOGRAPHY

The only biographical material is that given by the husband, Philip Stubbes, in *The Christall Glasse for Christian Women* (London, 1608). Short Title Catalog no. 176000. He is in the *Dictionary of National Biography*.

# The Four Daughters of Anthony Cooke

Four of the daughters of Anthony Cooke are of great interest because, in high station and learned in all of the skills of the Renaissance woman, they were not only committed to Anglican Protestantism, but strongly inclined toward Puritanism. The first was Anne, Lady Bacon, the mother of Francis Bacon; the second Mildred, Lady Burleigh, the wife of William Cecil, chief adviser to the queen for all of twoscore years. The third, Elizabeth, was first Lady Hoby, then Lady Russell, wife of John Russell, son of the Duke of Bedford. The fourth, Katherine, became Lady Killigrew. Her husband was a diplomat often abroad. While at Antwerp he supported the English Presbyterian congregation.[1]

## Katherine, Lady Killigrew

Let us move from the least to the better documented. Katherine, Lady Killigrew, was as highly lauded for her learning as were her sisters. After her death an admirer wrote, "Such was her mind, such excellence she bore, I once admired her, and I now deplore." Another wrote: "All Greece and Rome did in her numbers shine.

The sacred language too she made her own,
Nor eastern learning was to her unknown."

But of her literary output only a few Latin poems remain and in
English three stanzas, a playful plea to her sister, Lady Burleigh,
to employ her good offices to keep some gentleman from going
overseas:

If, Mildred, to my wishes kind
    Thy valued charge thou send,
In thee my soul shall own combined
    The sister and the friend.

If from my eyes by thee detained
    The wanderer cross the seas,
No more thy love shall sooth, as friend,
    No more as sister please.

His stay let Cornwall's shore engage;
    And peace with Mildred dwell;
Else war with Cecil's name I wage
    Perpetual war.—farewell.[2]

Engaging banter but nothing as to religion. Her stance can be
inferred from the letters of Edward Dering, the second husband
of Anne Locke.[3] He was a highly distinguished scholar and a
powerful preacher, so esteemed by his superiors as to be invited
in 1572 to preach before Queen Elizabeth. At the end of an edifying discourse he plunged into a tirade against the clergy, defiled
by trafficking in benefices. "Look at your ministers," said he to
the queen, "ruffians, hawkers, hunters, dicers, blind guides and
dumb dogs," some one and some another. This need not have
ruffled Elizabeth. She was not overpowered by esteem for the
clergy. He went on:

And yet you, in the meanwhile that all these whoredoms
are committed, you at whose hands God will require it, you
sit still and are careless. Let men do as they list. It toucheth
not belike your commonwealth, and therefore you are so
well contented to let all alone. The Lord increase the gifts
of his Holy Spirit in you, that from faith to faith you may

grow continually, till that you be zealous as good King David
to work his will. . . . Your Majesty must strengthen your
laws. . . . To keep back the ignorant from the ministry . . .
take away your authority from the bishops . . . Pull down
the court [of the archbishop], the mother and nurse of all
abominations. . . . Amend these horrible abuses. . . . God is
a righteous God, he will one day call you to your reckoning.
The God of all glory open your eyes to see his kingdom, and
enflame your heart to desire it.[4]

If the Queen could have brooked the personal rebuke she
might have been pleased with the substance of his recommenda-
tion, for what did it add up to if not the exaltation of the royal
supremacy? But exactly what did Dering have in mind? If the
bishops were to be shorn of authority, who would appoint the
ministers? The people? That would be Congregationalism. As-
sociations of ministers? That would be Presbyterianism. The
crown? That would be extreme Caesaropapism and what a task
for the government! Would the justices of the peace make the
appointments? Dering was inhibited from preaching, reinstated
and called before the court which he had dubbed, "the mother
and nurse of abominations."

He was examined on four counts:

1) Did he agree that the articles are in accord with the Word
of God? He replied that the Word of God had nothing about
the consecration of bishops.

2) Did he agree that the queen was the supreme governor in
matters ecclesiastical as well as civil? Yes.

3) Did he agree that there is nothing in the Prayer Book repugnant to the Word of God? Well, not exactly. The Word of God
does not call ministers priests.

4) Did he agree that the preaching of the Word in this Church
of England is sound and sincere? He couldn't say. He hadn't
heard all the sermons. And the sacraments: is the ministration
consonant with the Word of God? Not exactly. The Word does
not say that women may baptize, that the sign of the cross is to
be used in baptism or the wafer in the Eucharist. In addition he

was asked his opinion of the *Homilies* to be read by the clergy. He pointed out that they did not agree with the *Book of Common Prayer*, for they proscribe "pyping, singing, chaunting, playing open organs," which, they say, "displease God and defile his holy Temple." [5]

Nevertheless, said Dering, he had conformed out of deference to the will of the sovereign. He had worn the surplice and the cap, which he would not have done if given his liberty. He had used the *Book of Common Prayer* and had not absented himself from communion. His was a conformity of compliance along with sympathy for non-conformists. He was again inhibited, again restored. He grew more radical and would admit the royal supremacy only if the ruler were Christian. He might have ended his days in the Tower, but at the age of thirty-six he was carried off by tuberculosis.

This then was the man who wrote to Katherine Killigrew. His correspondence shows that he had been intimately in touch with her for a long time. Here are a few excerpts from the several letters [6] written before he was her husband.

It greeueth me good Mistris K. that you should be so long at Hendon as now you haue beene, and all this while I could finde no leisure to come vnto you, and whatsoeuer my fault hath beene heerein, I will make no other excuse, but desire you to forgiue it. And I pray God though I see you not, yet I may so remember you, as I am bound, and so my not cumming vnto you shall greeue me the lesse. Now touching your owne case, I know you are wise to see, that the Lord giueth you new instructions to bee wise in him, and to giue ouer your selfe vnto him. For as God hath blessed you many waies, and giuen you a good calling in the world, so he visiteth you every day, and humbleth you with many chastisements before him. God hath giuen you husband, children, family, and other blessings, but you enjoy none of them without a crosse, sometime in one thing, sometime in another, and commonly your owne weake and sickly body makes you that you cannot haue your ioy as you would.

The cross we learn was an unkind husband and a wayward son. Dering writes:

> Your sonne hath grieved you much, yea, but you haue not the hundreth part of the griefe that Dauid might haue had for his sonne Absolon: and will you be more grieued than he? Your sonne I trust shall yet proue well, and you shall see his recovery. . . . This griefe God recompenceth with great benefit, for our Sauiour Christ is our good warrant, that this is the lot of God's Saints, to enioy his blessings with afflictions, so that the more that you be sorrowfull, the more you be sure that the liuing God hath given you your portion: and so your sorrow is ioy vnto you. . . . The Lord bless you with his holy spirit, that you may in the midst of other care, haue pleasure in this, and in other sorrow reioyce in the Lord, and alwaies reioyce. Commend me I pray you, to your little ones, Nan, Besse & Mary. And the Lord make you and maister K. gladde parents of good children. Amen.

In the above excerpts he has addressed himself to her distresses. In another he is mindful of her help to him in his.

> I thanke you good Mistris K. for your Letter, and for your medicine, and for your good will to him to whom you before did owe so little. Touching my disease, I did suddainly cough & spit much blood, so that when with much forcing my selfe, I refrained, it ratteled in my throat, as if I had bin a dying: next day in the like sort I did, & once since the taking of these medicines for the staying of it. It is now staied, but I feele a great stopping of my wind, and much prouocation to cough, which if I did, I should spit blood as before. I pray you aske your Physition what hee thinketh best to be done. And good Mistris K. against all diseases and sicknesses of the bodie, doe as you do, and daily encrease it, with an vnfained testimony of your own hart. Commit your health, your sicknes, your body, your soule, your life, and your death, to the protection of him that died for vs, & is risen againe. A sicke body with such an aide, hath greater treasure then the Queenes Iewel house. Pray still, and pray for mee. I see the

goodnes of God such towardes mee, as (I thanke God) except
sinne, I weigh not all the world a feather: and with as glad
a minde I spitte blood, (I trust) as cleare spittle. To those
that love God, all things are for the best: he hath a hard
hart that beleeueth not this. . . . Commend mee to Maister K.
your little ones, to Maister R. The Lord blesse vs all, that
we make our bodies shake, and not our bodies vs. *Vale in
Christo Iesu. 25. Iul. 1575.*

*Tuus in Christo,* Ed. Dering.

Thus through a man there is disclosed to us a woman.

## *Elizabeth, first Lady Hoby, then Lady Russell*

Elizabeth, like her sister, is known to us through the men of
her family, though in her case not wholly. Her first husband,
during the persecution of Mary Tudor, spent much of his time
on the continent.[7] To this couple two sons were born. The first,
Edward, was under James I a scathing satirist of Roman claims.[8]
The second, called Thomas Posthumous Hoby, because born
after his father's death, pleased his mother by allowing no
dancing at his wedding.[9]

But there is more direct evidence as to her position. After she
had become Lady Russell we find this entry in the papers of
Queen Elizabeth:

Petition of Elizabeth, Dowager Lady Russell, Lord Hunsdon, and 29 other inhabitants of Blackfriars, London, to the
Council. One Burbage has lately bought rooms near Lord
Hunsdon's, and is converting them into a common playhouse, which will be a great annoyance to the neighbour-
hood, because of the gathering of vagrant and lewd persons,
on pretence of coming to the plays; because of its making

The Lady Hobbei.

The Holbein portrait of Lady Hoby from the Royal Library at Windsor Castle by permission of Her Majesty the Queen.

the place too populous, in case of a return of the sickness; and because the playhouse being near the church, the drums and trumpets will disturb divine service. There has not before been any playhouse in the precincts, but now that the Lord Mayor has banished the players from the city, they plant themselves in the liberties. Request that no playhouse may be kept there.[10]

More directly Lady Russell placed herself, perhaps unwittingly, in the stream of continental radical Protestantism by the translation of a tract which she entitled: *A Way of Reconciliation of a good and learned man, Touching the Trueth, Nature and substance of the Body and Blood of Christ in the Sacrament. Translated out of Latin into English by the Right Honorable Lady Elizabeth Russell Dowager to the Right Honorable the Lord John Russell, Baron and sonne and heire to Francis Earle of Bedford. Printed at London by RB.Anno 1605.*[11] The translation was dedicated to her daughter Nan, whom from the cradle, she had caused to "draw milk from the Holy Worde." Now by undertaking this translation she hoped to compose the dissensions among the Protestants over the interpretation of the Lord's Supper. All of their differences could be resolved if they would but recognize the distinction between the physical and the spiritual body of Christ. When the Lord said "This is my body," he had reference to the spiritual body. It is a real body and the Lutherans are perfectly right in saying that Christ is bodily present on the altar, but since the body is spiritual, feeding on him means receiving spiritual nourishment. This should satisfy the Zwinglians. Such was the argument.

Now where did this tract come from and who was the author? Elizabeth, in her preface, says that it was written in Germany about fifty years ago. Since her translation came out in 1605 this would be 1555. The work, she said, had been translated into French. Her title page says that she translated a Latin version. The translator from German into Latin assured the reader that he was not of the *parties* of the Anabaptists or Schwenckfelders. The name of the author was not divulged, "seeing that he was a man of great modesty." There was, however, a better reason to

A.

**Ayn kurtze gruntliche ahn-**
weisung zum rechten ver-
stande des Herzen Abent
mals oder h. Sacraments des leibs
vnnd blůts Christi/ vnnd wie es die
våtter vnnd allten Leerer der
Christlichen kirchen
haben vnder-
schaiden.

\*

1. Thess: 5.
Prüffet alles vnd was gůtte behaltet.

B.

**Eyn kurtzer**
gruntlicher bericht
zum rechten verstande
des Herten Christi
Nachtmals.

1561.

Title page of a tract by Caspar Schwenckfeld

suppress his name and give the assurance that the author was not a Schwenckfelder. The man who issued two tracts with this very same argument around 1554 and again in 1557 was none other than Caspar Schwenckfeld.[12] With good reason his name was concealed because, far from reconciling the parties, he had incurred the enmity of both. Luther and the Lutherans called him not Schwenckfeld, but *Stenckfeld* (Stinkfield), and the Zwinglians were equally caustic. Lady Russell was aligning herself with a group to the left of mainline Protestantism on the continent. Did she know it? Since she knew the date and that original was German, in all probability she did know that she was disseminating the views of Caspar Schwenckfeld.

One single sentence in her hand aligned her with English Protestantism to the left. The sentence was appended to a letter which she forwarded to her brother-in-law Lord Burghley. The author of the letter was Thomas Cartwright,[13] the man who gave a new turn to English Puritanism by shifting the emphasis from the rejection of vestments, which he was willing to wear, to the polity of the church of England. The norm for him was the pattern of the New Testament, which knew nothing of diocesan bishops. The word bishop then meant simply a pastor. The affairs of the church should be regulated by synods, that is presbyteries. Cartwright wished to fashion the Anglican church after the model of that in Scotland of which James I said, "No bishop, no king." He would have been right if he had said, "No bishop, no royal supremacy," for how could a monarch control the church if unable to appoint bishops who controlled the clergy?

Deprived of his professorship at Cambridge, Cartwright went to the continent. While in Holland he was pastor of a Presbyterian congregation organized at Antwerp with the help of Lord Killigrew. In 1582 Cartwright ventured to return to England. He was temporarily imprisoned at the insistence of the bishop of London, but was soon released and allowed to preach. Difficulties were soon created for him, however, because the Presbyterians began organizing conferences. Suspicion of fathering radical tracts and even of being the author of the outrageously amusing satires of Martin Marprelate led to his examination before the

High Commission. He was deliberately ambiguous lest he incriminate his brethren and refused to take the oath required.

In consequence he languished a long time in prison, while his wife was left to take care of five children of whom one died. He suffered from gout and sciatica. In this situation he invoked the intercession of Lady Russell.[14] He would not praise her unduly for her learning which is "not hable to resist the sieth (scythe) of death. . . . Godliness only is that which endureth." Neither would he unduly praise her for that, but "rather exhort you to further encrease therein . . ." But "I cannot passe by your singular and verie rare favour towards me . . . some five years past." He then recounts his grievances, that bail has not been allowed, though it is given to felons and recusant Papists. May she use her good offices with the Lord Treasurer (her brother-in-law, Burghley). To him she forwarded the letter with the one sentence which proves her to have been the patroness of English Puritans, "Good my Lord rede this thorow and do what you can to ye poore man."

He was released the next year.

## Anne, Lady Bacon

Lady Anne Bacon, the mother of two sons, Anthony and his renowned brother Francis, left no shadow of uncertainty about the intensity of her Protestant convictions. She was thoroughly agitated when her son Anthony employed the services of Catholics as well as Protestants in the interest of the crown. He had one familiar in particular whom she thoroughly detested and demanded his dismissal. Anthony asked a friend to mediate, but he reported that "it is as impossible to persuade my Lady as for myself to send you St. Paul's steeple."[15] The historian of Hertfordshire tells us that in this district she "gathered around her some of the most eminent of the Puritan ministers," a number of whom are named. The author surmises that the collection of Puritan documents entitled *A Parte of a Register* was issued at her expense and that she was the "Ladyship" to whom was dedicated *The Copie of a Letter with a Confession of Faith,* composed by two prominent Puritans.[16]

Her stance as to religion as well as her literary skill are evident in two translations and a letter from her pen. The first translation was entitled *Certayne Sermons of the ryghte famous and excellente clerk Master B. Ochine* and in another edition *Fouretene Sermons . . . concerninying the predestinacion and eleccion of God . . . Translated out of Italian . . . by A.C.*[17] The initials are those of Anne Cooke. Both editions are assigned to the year 1550. Ochino was an Italian exile, who prior to his defection from the Church of Rome, had been the general of the Capuchins and as a preacher, the Savonarola of his generation. After his apostasy he moved from center to left of center in his Protestantism and in all was banished from five countries.[18] A brief account of his early period is given in the first volume in this series. The material translated by Lady Bacon was quite in line with the prevailing Anglicanism.

The same was obviously true of her translation from the Latin of John Jewel's *Apology or Answer in Defense of the Church of England* a vindication of Canterbury against the Roman argument that the Protestants must be wrong because they did not agree among themselves. The rebuttal was: "Good God! What manner of fellows be these, which blames us for disagreeing? And do all they themselves, wean you, agree well?" Some wear shoes, some sandals, some linen, some wool, some white, some black, some are girt, some ungirt. "They were best therefore, to go and set peace at home rather among their own selves. Of a truth unity and concord doth best become religion; yet is not unity the sure and certain mark whereby to know the church of God, for there was the greatest consent that might be amongst them that worshipped the golden calf." [19]

Lady Bacon's translation met with the unqualified approval of Jewel, and Archbishop Parker wrote a commendatory preface. He hoped that by her example "all noble gentlewomen would be allured from vain delights to doing of more perfect glory."

Thus far Lady Bacon was entirely in line with the official forms of the Reformation, but in a private letter her Puritan leanings found expression. The occasion was a communication in 1587 of the Commons to the "Lordes spiritual and temporal" that among other points the ministers should be more numerous, they should not be troubled for the omission of some portions from the Book of Common Prayer, they should not be called before the High Commission save for "notable offenses" and they should be permitted to have "exercises and conferences among themselves." [20] The "exercises" referred presumably to the "prophesyings," gatherings of both clergy and laity for the exposition and discussion of Scripture. The word "conferences" will have referred to the Presbyterian synods. The queen had demanded their suppression because such discussions "lead to divided opinions upon pointes of divinity farre unmeete for vulgar people." Archbishop Grindal refused to use his authority to forbid them, for he found them instructive for the clergy and edifying for the laity. The queen suspended him from his functions. His death saved her from the embarrassment of deposition.[21] After him came the more rigorous Whitgift. The response to the petition by the lords spiritual was to petition the queen not to relax her policy of suppression. Nor did she.

Lady Bacon then addressed her brother-in-law, Lord Burghley, with the plea that the "faithful ministers" be granted the opportunity to present their case in person to the queen. She added her testimony to the benefit she had derived from the exercises. She wrote, "For mine own part, my good Lord, I will not deny, but as I may hear them in their public exercises as a chief duty commanded by God to widows, and also I confess as one that hath found mercy, that I have profited more in the inward feeling knowledge of God his holy will, though but in a small measure, by such sincere and sound opening of the Scriptures by an ordinary preaching within these seven or eight years, than I did by hearing odd sermons at Paul's well-nigh twenty years together." [22]

Burghley's efforts were unavailing. Elizabeth had her way and her successors reaped the whirlwind.

## *Mildred, Lady Burghley*

Mildred, Lady Burghley, was no less renowned than her sisters for learning, and was even preferred to them by a Latin poet, Ockland by name, who composed a panegyric on Queen Elizabeth and dedicated it to Lady Burghley

> that very noble and highly erudite lady, versed alike in Latin and Greek, the Lady Mildred, wife of the great Lord Treasurer Burghley. There were many learned women in Greece whose works, drawn from the wells of Parnassus, are extant, but how much more remarkable is the mastery of Greek by those in distant lands, who, after learning their own vernacular, have by diligent labor, acquired a knowledge of both Greek and Latin, thus combining Homer and Virgil! Of the four illustrious sisters I turn to you Mildred that you may be my Pallas to shield me from acrimonious criticism. I know that my verses are not equal to the virtue of my queen. I hope the reader will not view them with a jaundiced eye. My lines I entrust to your tutelage and hope you will not spurn your suppliant." [23]

All of this teaches us nothing, of course, as to Mildred's religious opinions, and as a matter of fact, very little has been recorded in detail. The Scotch Presbyterians were confident of her sympathy and support. There are several letters to her from William Maitland, Laird of Lyddington, telling her that Lord James and he thanked her for her "furtherance of this common cause," and trusting that she will not "wexe cold." [24]

The Spanish ambassador was in no doubt as to where she stood. The occasion was the proposed marriage of Elizabeth with the Duke of Austria, a Roman Catholic. The ambassador communicated to his government that "Cecil seems to desire this business so greatly that he does not speak about the religious point, but this may be deceit, as his wife is of the contrary opinion and thinks that great trouble may be caused to the peace of the country through it. She has great influence with her husband,

and no doubt discusses the matter with him, but she appears a much more ferocious heretic than he is." [25]

Conyers Read, in his magnificent study of Lord Burghley, remarks that during the last thirty years of his marriage to Mildred not a single letter between them has survived. We do have his tribute when she was taken. I quote a portion followed by Read's summary.[26]

'Therefore my cogitation ought to be occupied in these things following:

'To thank Almighty God for his favour, in permitting her to live so many years together with me, and to have given her grace to have had the true knowledge of her salvation by the death of her son, Jesus, opened to her by the knowledge of the gospel, whereof she was a professor from her youth.

'I ought to comfort myself with the remembrance of her many virtues and godly actions wherein she continued all her life. And specially in that she did of late years sundry charitable deeds whereof she determined to have no outward knowledge while she lived. In so much as when I had some little understanding thereof, and asked her wherein she had disposed any charitable gifts (according to her often wishing that she were able to do some special act for maintenance of learning and relief of the poor), she would always only show herself rather desirous so to do than ever confess any such act. As since her death is manifestly known to me and confessed by sundry good men (whose names and ministries she secretly used) that she did charge them most strictly that while she lived they should never declare the same to me nor to any other.

'And so now have I seen her earnest writings to that purpose of her own hand. The particulars of many of these hereafter do follow, which I do with mine own handwriting recite for my own comfort in the memory thereof, with assurance that God hath accepted the same in such favourable sort as she findeth now the fruits thereof in heaven.'

He then proceeded to enumerate Mildred's benefactions, concluding "And wool and flax for poor women in Chesnut, to be wrought into cloth and given to the poor."

In this enumeration of her charities there is nothing to mark her as a Protestant, let alone a Puritan. We have here rather an example of what Jordan has called the "secularization of philanthropy." [27] A better expression would be the laicization of philanthropy. What had happened was that the resources of the state had been dissipated by wars and the resources of the church despoiled by the state. Neither was in a position to relieve the poor. Private philanthropy stepped in. The chief givers were the London merchants and the London merchants were the core of the Puritan party. Her example does illustrate the introduction of a vast social change under the impact of a particular situation and a particular religious ethic.

## NOTES

### Katherine, Lady Killigrew

STC is Short Title Catalogue

1. A. F. Scot Pearson, *Thomas Cartwright* (Cambridge, 1925), 172-3.
2. George Ballard, *Memoirs of British Ladies* (London, 1875), 142-7.
3. Edward Dering appears in the DNB. He is briefly treated in Leonard J. Trinterud, *Elizabethan Puritanism* (New York, 1971), where his *Sermon before the Queen* is reproduced and a letter to Mrs. Barret, but not those to Lady Killigrew. Dering appears repeatedly in M. M. Knappen, *Tudor Puritanism* (Chicago, 1939), third impression 1970. There is a good sketch in Pearson, *op. cit.*
4. Trinterud, *op. cit.*, pp. 159-60.
5. *A Parte of a Register* (Edinburgh, 1593), a copy in the Beinecke library of Yale University in which is inserted a photostat of an appendix.
6. *Certaine godly and comfortable Letters* in his *Workes* (London, 1614), Beinecke library of Yale, *STC* 6678.

### Elizabeth, Lady Hoby, Later Lady Russell

7. Hoby, Thomas in *DNB* and Christina Garrett, *Marian Exiles* (1938).
8. His tracts *STC* 13539 and 13540, both in Beinecke Lbrary, Yale.
9. George Ballard, *Memoirs of British Ladies* (London, 1875), pp. 137-8. Dorothy M. Meads, *Diary of Lady Margaret Hoby* (London, 1930), p. 34.

10. *Calendar of State Papers, Elizabeth, Domestic* 1595-97, CCLX, No. 116, p. 310.
11. *STC* 21456.
12. *Corpus Schwenckfeldianorum* XIV, Doc. 912 and XV, Doc. 1021, p. 372.
13. A. F. Scot Pearson, *Thomas Cartwright* (Cambridge, 1925).
14. *Ibid.,* app. XXIX.
15. James Spedding, *The Letters and Life of Francis Bacon,* London 1861, Vol. I, p. 3.
16. William Urwick, *Nonconformity in Hertfordshire,* London 1884, p. 86.
17. A copy of *Certaine Sermons* can be found in the Beinecke Library of Yale University containing 25 sermons of which 12-25 inclusive are the work of Anne Cooke.
18. See my *Bernardino Ochino,* Florence 1940, together with a briefer account in English in *Travail of Religious Liberty,* Westminster Press 1951.
19. *The Works of John Jewel,* vol. III, Parker Society 1848, pp. 68f.
20. Thomas Fuller, *The Church History of Britain,* Oxford 1845, vol. V, bk. IX, cent. 16 sec. 7.
21. Stanford E. Lemberg, 'Archbishop Grindal and the Prophesyings', *Historical Magazine of the Protestant Episcopal Church* XXXIV, 1965, pp. 87-145.
22. Spedding, *op. cit.,* pp. 40-42.
23. *EIRHNARXIA Sive Elizabetha,* London 1582, in the Beinecke Library of Yale University.
24. Samuel Haynes, *Collection of State Papers . . . left by William Cecil,* London 1740-59, vol. I, pp. 293, 301, & 359.
25. *Calendar of State Papers. Spanish 1558-67,* p. 580.
26. Conyers Read, *Lord Burghley and Queen Elizabeth,* New York 1960, p. 447.
27. W. K. Jordan, *Philanthropy in England 1480-1660,* London 1959.

# DENMARK

## Queen Dorothea and Anna Hardenberg

For Denmark the only women I have been able to discover in this period with profound religious involvement are two queens and one noblewoman. The first is Isabel (Elizabeth), the queen of Christian II. She was a Hapsburg, a sister of Charles V, Ferdinand of Austria, Maria of Hungary and Eleanor of Portugal. Of all the members of her family she alone was an avowed Lutheran. She has already received treatment briefly in our first volume, in connection with her residence in Wittenberg, and will therefore be omitted here.

The second queen is Dorothea,[1] the wife of Christian III. Both husband and wife were ardently Lutheran. Their coronation ritual was composed by Luther's associate, Bugenhagen. One is puzzled to read that it was written in German in order to be understood. Why not Danish? The answer is that during the preceding period the Danish nobility had been so weakened by feuds that the king's primary support came from the German element in his constituency. He was accused of seeking to Germanize Denmark. Such was not so much his intent as his necessity.[2] In his correspondence with the Lutherans in Germany he used also their tongue rather than Latin.

The coronation ceremony is strictly Lutheran.[3] The queen is instructed that her head is to be covered. That, of course, could be equally Catholic. Was the point specified to insist that the affair was religious rather than secular? The king and queen are

King Christian III and Queen Dorothea

exhorted to promote the holy gospel in perpetuity. Let them provide for the poor, found hospitals and pay the salaries of teach-
ers and ministers lest the people degenerate into Turks. The
promise of care for the ministers is repeated in each of the oaths.

The religious opinions of the pair are better known for the
husband than for the wife, because we have his letters to the
German theologians.[4] He assures them of his great concern for
the pure teaching, the observance of the sacraments, the cure of
souls. He laments the death of that blessed man of God, Martin
Luther, and announces measures for the dissemination of his
works in Denmark. Deviations from strict Lutheranism are not to
be tolerated and Christian III rejoices that the blasphemous
Servetus had been put out of the way. Whether his wife approved
of burning at the stake we do not know.

Her letters are chiefly to members of the family and in German.[5] They are full of godly admonitions of the sort that might
equally well have been composed by a Catholic. Two sons gave
her particular concern. Magnus, the younger, appears to have
been an alcoholic. Frederick, the elder and heir to the throne,
elicited on that account special solicitude. On December 18,
1558 she wrote him, "My dearly beloved son: I have received two
of your letters of late and rejoice that you are in good health.
May the merciful God lead you in the paths of righteousness to
the welfare of your subjects. My mother's heart cannot conceal
from you that your father is very weak, and so . . ." The *and so*
meant that the son's uneasy head would soon wear the crown.[6]

A fortnight later, three days before the death of the king (Jan.
1, 1559), came another letter fraught with the gravest concern
over the son's behavior. "My dearly beloved son: As to what you
tell me about Anna I cannot conceal my concern. To destroy
another's happiness is something for which I cannot answer to
God. I well know that our life here below is very brief, but in
the beyond everlasting. I know you are honorable and would
not wish to deprive another of happiness. My heart is so troubled
that I cannot say more." [7]

The Anna in question was a lady in waiting at the court with
whom the prince was infatuated. The mother's reference to
destroying another's happiness could not have been to Anna,

A portion of a letter from Queen Dorothea to her son Frederick about to become Frederick II (Dec. 18, 1558).

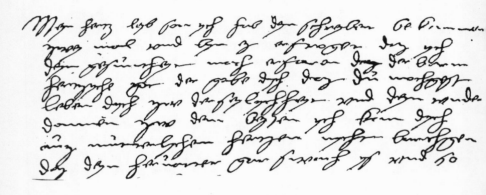

Meyn hertz leyb son, ych hab deyn schreiben bekommen zwey mal und byn es erfroget, das ych deyn gesuntheyt mach erfaren der barm herztzyche got der gebe dych das du mochgest leben dych zu der seylychheit vnd deyn vnderdannen zu dem besten, ych kan dych ausz mutterlychen hertzen nycht barchgen das deyn her 'uatter gar schwach ys und so . . . .

### Translation

"My very dear son: I have received two of your letters and am very happy that you are in good health. May the merciful God lead you in the paths of righteousness to the welfare of your subjects. My mother's heart cannot withhold from you that your father is very weak and so . . ."

The "and so" intimated that Frederick's would soon be "the uneasy head that wears the crown."

who was equally enamored, but rather to the young man to whom she was betrothed, and probably even more to his family, who presumably had made all the arrangements. Such a betrothal in that day was deemed well nigh as binding as a marriage. In all probability another consideration weighed with Dorothea, that a crown prince should not be expended on a lady in waiting however honorable, but rather utilized for a political union with a queen or princess. Frederick answered that he quite understood his mother's concern.[8] He resolved that if he could not have Anna he would have no one. She, too, renounced the betrothal and remained single. So they continued for a decade.

During that period Dorothea did her best to arrange an advantageous match for her son with Queen Elizabeth of England, Mary Queen of Scots, Renata of Lorraine or an Austrian princess. Frederick was obdurate. Then after ten years the king, knowing that such a marriage might entail abdication, not to mention distress to his mother, married Anna Hardenberg. What impelled the couple to this act of defiance? I have suggested that the Reformation by individualizing faith personalized marriage. Two Danish authoresses suggest another aspect of the Reformation.[9] The movement itself, they point out, was a revolt against authority. When the queen repudiated the authority of the pope why should not they repudiate the authority of the queen? This is an interesting inversion of the psychiatric explanation of the origin of the Reformation on the ground that Luther in order to be somebody in his own right broke first with the authority of his father and then with that of the church in order to found one of his own. Factually this is invalid, but it is theoretically possible that a revolt against parents might lead to revolt against the church and also that a revolt against the church might lead to a revolt against parents. The Reformation was, indeed, a revolutionary movement, involving new patterns of behavior in religion, politics and domestic relations.

But now, after only four years, the union of Frederick and Anna was dissolved. What could have happened? My first thought, when I knew only the bare facts, was that two persons so unflinchingly defiant of the ethos of the times were too rigidly independent to get along with each other. Some of Anna's friends, however, saw in Frederick's repudiation a plain case of infidelity to the vow, "till death do us part." [10] I, too, might have thought so had I not received from Denmark the book which publishes Anna's confidential letters. Then I saw that the difficulty lay in Anna's inability during four years to provide an heir to the throne. Frederick had the sagacity to see that if the succession were not established Denmark might be embroiled in civil war between rival factions of the nobility. His situation was precisely that of Henry VIII. But yet not quite precisely. Denmark was a Lutheran country and there was no need to be entangled in canon law and embroiled with the pope. To obtain a divorce Anna would not have to confess that for four years they had lived in sin.

She, too, perceived the gravity of the situation, and this couple, so adamant in rejecting the current view in domestic relations, when the welfare of the state was involved, renounced their personal desires. She wrote to an intimate friend, "The king is making over to me a thousand dollars *(tussind daller,* no small sum then.) He tells me he knows I am godfearing and commends me to God's care. He assures me he loves me dearly *(loffed meg harti)."* [11] In all the letters of Anna there is not a hint of recrimination.

Frederick, after a year, married his fifteen-year-old cousin Sophia of Mecklenberg and she enabled him to fulfill the needs of state. Anna also remarried. The close friend in whom she confided was the one to whom our next sketch is devoted, Birgitte Gjøe.

## NOTES

1. The *Danske Biografisk Lexikon* has brief accounts of Dorothea and Frederick II. There is a fuller account of her by Ellen Jørgensen og Johanne Skovgaard, *Danske Dronninger* (Copenhagen, 1910), 96-115.

2. Dietrich Schäfer, *Geschichte von Dänmark* (Gotha, 1895), the chapter "Christians III Verwaltung."

3. Friederich C. C. H. Münter, *Akstykker vedkommende Kong Christian den Tredies og Dronning Dorotheas Kroning* . . . i Kjøbenhavn den 12te Aug. 1537 af Dr. J. Bugenhagen . . . 1831.

4. Martin Schwarz Lausten, "König Christian III von Dänemark und die Deutschen Reformation," *Archiv für Reformationsgeschichte* LXVI (1975), 151-81.

5. and 6. See the list of illustrations for p. 120.

7. Carl Frederick Bricke, *Konig Frederick den andens Ungdomskjaerlighed et historisk Forsøg* (Copenhagen, 1873), p. 42, note 1.

8. *Ibid.*, p. 44.

9. Jørgensen, note 1 above.

10. Bricka, *op. cit.*, Letter No. 24.

11. *Ibid.*, Letters 31 and 34, pp. 226-7.

Birgitte Gjøe

# Birgitte Gjøe
## (1511-1574)

Birgitte Gjøe is of interest by reason of her ardent Lutheranism and her administration of an influential school, modeled along the lines initiated by Melanchthon. She was a lady-in-waiting to Queen Dorothea and the wife of the Lord High Admiral, Herluf Trolle. The husband, as so often, is better documented than the wife. We have two volumes of their correspondence, including some of his to her but none of hers to him. Perhaps while with the fleet he had no filing cabinet.

He was a staunch Lutheran who had studied at Wittenberg and there had formed a life long friendship with a fellow student, Niels Hemmingsen, later to be the foremost Lutheran preacher in Denmark. The Lord High Admiral certainly took his religion seriously and founded the school above mentioned. At the same time he appears to have been a bit of a card in view of the way he recast the family coat of arms into his bookplate. The figure above has more of a leering tongue. A leaf on the left becomes a sinister beast and the headless chap below is more animated. The pelican's beak in place of a helmet is a sheer innovation. Was he just poking fun at heraldry?

Our primary concern is with his wife. Her mother died when Birgitte was in infancy. The father remarried and the stepmother shipped the child off to a convent. There she imbibed Lutheran teaching, insinuated clandestinely, we may be sure, as in other instances already noticed. After the death of the stepmother Bir-

gitte lived for a time with sisters, then joined the household of
the queen, by whom the Lutheran inclinations would have been
strengthened. As to Birgitte's education, we are left to inference
from a letter to her from a minister who sprinkled his Danish
with Greek and finished with a piece of rather esoteric erudition which he assumed she would understand. He concluded by
saying that he was writing on the 25th of March, the day on
which Adam sinned, the flood was deluged upon the earth, the
Savior was conceived by the Virgin Mary and on which he died
to save us from our sins.

The chronological details arose from the attempt to give the
gospel a cosmic setting. The nativity was set on December 25th,
the winter solstice on the old reckoning. The conception fell
therefore nine months earlier on March 25th, the spring equinox. As for the dates of the crucifixion and resurrection, there
had been much controversy in the early church, with unwilling-
ness to run the risk of turning Christ into a rising and dying
nature god if his resurrection were made to coincide with that
of Attis on the equinox. The Council of Nicea ruled that Easter
should be celebrated on the first Sunday—that was Christian—
after the first full moon—The Jewish year was lunar—after the
vernal equinox. How Adam's fall and the flood were brought
into the scheme I do not know. The writer apparently assumed
that Birgitte would.

The letters from her husband disclose little about her religious position. He begins always by addressing her as "Darling
sweetheart" and concludes by commending her to God's unfail-
ing keeping. Religion for this pair was not a problem to be
discussed, but a life to be lived. He does not probe into the im-
plications of justification by faith, but tells her about a naval
battle with the Swedes and asks her to arrange for the transport
of a keg of wine.

There is a point in her career which offers another illustration
of revolt against family-made marriages. The stepmother forced
upon Birgitte an engagement when only fourteen. She objected.
So also did the young man. Both submitted during the lifetime
of the stepmother and signed the certificates of agreement which
were deemed as binding as a marriage. When the overbearing

parent died, the couple contrived to have the contract nullified and in due time Birgitte married Herluf. They had together a very happy partnership for twenty-one years. She survived him for nine years and busied herself with the administration of the school, which a modern historian of the university of Copenhagen treats as a forerunner. The curriculum was the work of her husband's old friend, Niels Hemmingsen, who has been called the Melanchthon of Denmark.

Coat of Arms and Bookplate of Herluf Trolle

## BIBLIOGRAPHY

Both Birgitte and Herluf Trolle are in the *Dansk Biografisk Lexikon.* There is a full biography of him with a chapter on her by E. Briand Crèvecoeur, *Herluf Trolle* (Jørgen Sandal, Denmark, 1959). The letter about March 25th is given by T. A. Becker, "Herluf Trolle og Birgitte Goye," *Kerkhistorie Samliger* (Copenhagen, 1864-66), p. 577. The two volumes of letters are edited by G. L. Wad, *Breve til og fra Herlof Trolle og Birgitte Gjøe,* I-II (1893), (borrowed from the Library of Congress.) The history of the University of Copenhagen, which pays a tribute to the Herlufsholm school is by Holger Fr. Rordam, *Kjøbenhavns Universitets Historie* II (1864-72), p. 446.

# NORWAY

# *Anna Pedersdotter Absalon*

Anna Pedersdotter Absalon is one of the most renowned women
from Norway of the olden days. At least so I have been told.
She was burned as a witch in the year 1590. Her repute may well
be due in part to the treatment accorded her by a distinguished
Norwegian playwright, Wiers-Hanssen. John Masefield turned it
into English and his version of *The Witch* had a considerable
run in New York and London.[1]

The story as related in the play is that Absalon Beyer, in his
sixties, became infatuated with the lovely Anna Pedersdotter in
her twenties. Her hand was obtained through pressure exerted by
her mother out of gratitude to him for having saved her from
being burned as a witch by the fanatical Lutherans. He knew the
charge to be true but dissimulated. After five years of the marriage, Absalon's son by a former wife, came home and he and
Anna were soon infatuated. When a cronie of Anna's mother
was charged with sorcery, this time Absalon did not lie and she
was burned. Stricken in conscience over his earlier duplicity,
Absalon disclosed the whole to his son and Anna, whose love for
each other was evident. He admitted he had wronged her. She
flared up and upbraided him for stealing five years of her youth
and depriving her of motherhood. She confided to her lover the
wish that the father were dead that they might be free. He died
suddenly. At his bier his mother, who had always hated Anna,
taxed her with sorcery in bewitching the son and killing the

father. Anna, who had come to doubt herself, admitted the charge. The sequel is left to inference. Powerful drama, distorted history! Two points only are correct. She was married to Absalon and she did die as a witch. But she was not an unwilling wife for five years, rather a devoted partner of twenty-three years. She was not deprived of a child. There was at least one son. She was not burned by fanatical Lutherans, but by a civil tribunal against the protest of the Lutheran clergy.

Before turning to the real Anna Absalon, a word is in order as to why she should be introduced at all in a series on the role of women in the religious movements of the age of the Reformation. She is the only example which brings in witchcraft. The theme is relevant with respect to the general attitude toward women, since the opinion is current that witch hunting was an aspect of anti-feminism. To a degree it was. The word witch is feminine and a manual on witches in the fifteenth century explained that women are the more easily seduced by Satan because more credulous, impressionable, garrulous and frail.[2] A modern historian finds the explanation rather in that women, because of menstruation, were associated with the moon, which presides over the realm of darkness.[3] No doubt more women suffered on the score of witchcraft than men, but there were male counterparts, known variously as warlocks, wizards, magicians, sorcerers and necromancers. In 1590, the very year of the burning of Anna, a man in Trier suffered in like manner. Dietrich Flade was a judge in the witch trials. The accused plead guilty and then incriminated the judge himself, whom they claimed to have seen in attendance at their sabbaths.[4]

Ordinarily the connection was not immediate between witch hunting and the religious issues. Indirectly one may surmise that the upheavals of the wars of religion, the exiles of populations, the executions for heresy begat a suspicion of sinister forces. In the case of Anna, however, the connection was direct. She was the wife of Absalon Pederson Beyer, Norway's most illustrious humanist scholar at the time and also a theologian and clergyman. For two years he had studied under Melanchthon at Wittenberg. Until his death in 1574 Absalon lectured in theology at the Cathedral School of Bergen and was also pastor to the governor general of the province.[5]

Absalon was a fervid Protestant who supported the clergy in the destruction of images. The town council had for some time been sensitive to the spoliation and demolition of churches for reason of finance and defense. The cathedral at Bergen and other churches were demolished on the plea that the space was needed for ramparts. Then came religious iconoclasm.[6] The Lutherans took over the *Kors Kirke* and the *Maria Kirke*. They would allow crucifixes, but not images of Mary and the saints. When, then, the Lutheran bishop, with the concurrence of Beyer, removed the images from the high altar the council was incensed. Since the bishop and Absalon were too entrenched to be removed, they were struck by charging their wives with witchcraft. Both were exonerated by the court. This was in 1575, the year after Absalon's death.

Fifteen years later the case was reopened because a local family objected to the marriage of their daughter to the son of Anna, who, despite vindication by the court, could never cast off the suspicion of her neighbors. The case was reopened. We have the records of her trial before a civil tribunal in a modern critical edition. The *Retsakten*[7] (Acts of the trial) begin with a list of the names of the judges, nearly all ending in sønn: Olssønn, Hanssønn, Jakopssønn, Biornnssøn and so and so's sønn, thirty-eight persons in all, and not a woman among them. But those who gave testimony against Anna were women. Was this feminine anti-feminism?

We have the testimony of Anna Snidkers, who had a grudge against Anna Absalon for having brought her to prison on a charge of witchcraft of which she was cleared. Now her husband, Giertt, was a cabinet maker who refused, prior to payment, to deliver a weaving frame to Anna Absalon. She fumed, stomped into the house, accompanied by a headless boy in black. She swore to knock out Anna Snidkers, who thereupon fainted and for three days was in a coma. On recovering her senses she vomited "unnatural matter," such as feathers, hair, threads and pins. She was rather uncomfortable for some time after and for this held Anna Absalon alone responsible. Anna Snidkers again be-

came sick and died and for this also she blamed Anna Absalon
(posthumously?)

Testimony was given by another Giertt, the husband of Jhanichenn, to the effect that Anna had come to have his wife change
some Norwegian dollars into Danish currency to be sent to her
son. A dollar fell at the feet of Jhanichenn, who, bending down
to pick it up, was seized by an unusual sickness. She asked her
husband whether he had ever had a quarrel with Anna. He said
that once she had sent for some wine which was not sent, then
for beer which was not sent, then for vinegar. One present exclaimed, "For Jesus' sake let her have it and put the money in
the poor box." (Perhaps the translation should be "in the poor
box in the name of Jesus," thus forefending sorcery). This was
done and Jhanichenn died.

We have next the case of a lad of about four years, carried on
his mother's arm. Anna offered him a cookie. He shook his head.
His mother told him to take it. He bit and was stricken by an
illness which made him black in the face, stiff as a log and so
heavy his mother had to sit down. After a time he died in pain.
Anna's response to this was that many children were dying in
Bergen. Was she responsible for them all? The editor notes that
women of the lower classes under examination were dazed and
dumb. Anna had wits and spirit.

Next the mayor presented the confessions of two women
previously executed for witchcraft, who, when on trial, had
claimed that Anna was more adept in the art of necromancy
than they. She had been with them at the witches' sabbath on
the eve of a holy day. Anna Snidkers' claim was confirmed that
she had died because of Anna's hex. Marenn Jacobsdotter said
that Anna had appeared in the cassock of a priest or the cowl of
a monk to work the death of the bishop in order that her
husband might succeed him (ecclesiastical politics enter).

The most damning testimony came from Anna's maid, Elena,
who on oath said that during her twenty years of service she
had come to know of the witchcraft of Anna Absalon, by whom
she had been turned into a horse and ridden to the witches'
sabbath on the mountain called Lyderhorn. Before Anna mounted, Elena twice champed her bit. Elena was very young and did

Riding to the witches' sabbath on a goat. Often the witch was shown riding on a broom. That she should transform a person into a horse for a steed was not out of line with current belief.

The Most High Lord of the Witches

not exactly understand what was going on. On arrival at the mountain she was tethered with other horses. A great crowd gathered and resolved to cause all the ships arriving at Bergen that year to sink and perish. On a second occasion the decision was to burn Bergen to the ground. There came a great thunder storm on Christmas day in the morning, as we all know. On a third occasion the vicious assembly decided to swallow Bergen in a flood. Thereupon appeared a man in white raiment with a wand who said the Mighty Highest Lord would not allow it and dispersed the concourse. Elena further testified that she and Anna on their return were very tired and received the sacrament.

Anna branded all of this as sheer lies, said she had never been at the Lyderhorn and didn't know where it was (though, says the recorder, every one could see it from Bergen). Since two of Elena's statements were true, that there had been a thunder storm and that she and Anna had taken the sacrament, the remainder of her testimony was deemed trustworthy. Anna was condemned by a secular tribunal and burned in 1590. Six years later her son petitioned the king to reverse the verdict, which tarnished the reputation of the family. The king, after two years, upheld the condemnation (1598).

## NOTES

1. John Masefield, *The Witch* (New York, 1926).
2. *Malleus Maleficarum* of Kramer and Sprenger in 1486, passages in English by Julia O'Faolain and Lauro Martines, *Not in God's Image* (Harper & Row Torchbooks (1973).
3. Julio Caro Barofa, *The World of Witches,* tr. Glendenning (New York, 1933), pp. 7-12, 39-40.
4. George Lincoln Burr, "The Fate of Dietrich Flade" (1890), reprinted in Bainton and Gibbons, *George Lincoln Burr* (Cornell, 1943).
5. Jergen Theodore Jorgenson, *History of Norwegian Literature* (New York, 1933), pp. 123-26.
6. Thomas B. Willson, *History of the Church and State in Norway from the Tenth to the Sixteenth Century* (Westminster, England, 1971).
7. Bente Gullveig Alver, *Hekstro og Troldom* (Oslo, 1971), pp. 81-110. For help in reading the acts of the trial in sixteenth century Norwegian I am indebted to Sigred Osberg of Bergen and Professor and Mrs. Nils Dahl of the Yale Divinity School.

Bona Sforza at her marriage

# POLAND

## *Bona Sforza*

If this volume moved consistently clockwise around the circumference of Europe Poland should not come before Sweden, but the queen of Sweden was the daughter of the queen of Poland and mothers do come first. Bona Sforza [1] is not the only woman chosen to represent Poland. The entire roster exhibits a greater social range than we have seen elsewhere and a wider cultural diversity, since Bona came from abroad and intensified the Italian influence. In her ancestry she included Italy, both north and south, and also Spain.[2] Her father was Galeazzo Maria Sforza, duke of Milan. Her mother was half a Sforza—the parents were cousins—and half Spanish, the daughter of Alonso of Aragon. His holdings were in southern Italy, for he was the Duke of Rossano in Calabria and king of Naples.

The period was that of the Renaissance, the age of the despots, a time of literary efflorescence, artistic genius, and secularist tendencies in the highest circles of the church. When Isabella, by marriage to Gian Galeazzo Sforza, became the duchess of Milan a masque was staged in her honor. She appeared magnificently attired, resplendent with jewels, vying with the sun. Actors costumed as stars and planets revolved in their orbits, while chanting her praises. Then Apollo brought the three muses and seven virtues to present a volume of tributes. The designer of this masque was Leonardo da Vinci. Another eminent artist in this circle was Bramante.[3]

But Isabella was not happy in Milan. Her husband was over-shadowed by his uncle, Ludovico Moro, who, when Gian was little, had been made regent and was not inclined to relinquish power. And Ludovico's sparkling wife, Beatrice d'Este, though only the duchess of Bari, outshone in the brilliance of her court, the very duchess of Milan.[4] Isabella complained to her father.[5]

Her husband died at the age of twenty-five. Isabella clad her four children in black. They rebelled.[6] Thus early Bona showed spunk. There was suspicion of poison. There always was in the case of a sudden death, especially if any one stood to gain by it and Ludovico did. He promptly had himself made duke instead of continuing as regent for Isabella's little boy. Beatrice d'Este became the duchess of Milan and Isabella was made the duchess of Bari. She took her children and went to her father in Naples. Then after a time assumed her functions as duchess of Bari. By that time the only one of her children remaining was Bona.[7]

Her education was continued in the Neapolitan circle, no less devoted to the new learning than that of Milan. Bona was given the most competent instruction in all of those disciplines deemed appropriate for a high lady of the Renaissance: music, dancing, familiarity with the classics and competence in Latin. Bona's grandmother and mother wrote it and no doubt spoke it excellently. Among the humanists of Naples, one met again that blending of the classical and the Christian which made one wonder whether paganism was christianized or Christianity paganized. The Neapolitan poet Sannazaro pictured the Virgin reading the Sibylline Oracles at the time of the Annunciation and mingled the gods of Olympus and the denizens of hades with the Wise Men and the shepherds.[8]

A tract by a woman, a friend of Bona's mother,[9] blended more subtly the pagan and the Christian. Not gods but ideas were mingled. The title was *De Vera Tranqvillita d'Animo (On True Peace of Mind)*. The first prescription was the Cynic formula, to divest oneself in advance of everything of which one could be deprived. Live like a dog. The word Cynic is derived from the Greek word for dog. Imitate Diogenes. The second prescription was taken from the Stoics. Let reason hold in leash all of those passions and emotions which agitate the spirit: anger, rage, vindictiveness, ambition, pride. Listen to Zeno. Then came the Christian answer. "Hold before your eyes that sweet spouse of our souls, Christ crucified. He was naked to clothe you, imprisoned to free you. Look upon his pierced hands, his head crowned with thorns to be crowned with glory. Our joy stems from his pain, our health from his weakness, our life from his death of which through him we have no longer fear." There is the recognition that the Christian must suffer divers ills including the infirmities of age. Every one desires to reach a ripe age but no one is pleased to be congratulated on having achieved it. Poor girl, what did she know of old age? Her sage observation was taken from Cicero. The tract is not basically Christian, for there is no recognition that one must not only bear adversity with fortitude but must also assume the cross.

More influential on the development of Bona that Sannazaro or the author of this tract was undoubtedly her mother Isabella. She would instill in her daughter no profound piety.[10] To be sure Isabella practiced her devotions and went on pilgrimages. They were often a lark. But in her we find none of those agonies and ecstasies of spirit common to her friends, Vittoria Colonna and Giulia Gonzaga. Isabella was an activist, who relished the opportunity afforded by Bari for the exercise of that genius for administration for which there had been no scope at Milan. She is said to have been more feared than loved because of the tight efficiency which supplied Bari with a canal, a bridge and improved fortifications.[11] No talk on her part about bearing the cross!

Yet there was one point at which she took it for granted. Children were not to indulge their fancies as to mates. Bona understood that she must comply with parental choice even if there were a cross. A young suitor was enamored of her beauty. Her word to him was that she could do him no greater good than to have nothing to do with him.[12] Well she perceived that the duchess of Bari, the one time duchess of Milan, would not allow her only surviving child to be squandered on a mere *galant'uomo*.

Negotiations for an advantageous match was started early. They always were. One plan was that the mother Isabella should be married to Francis I of Francis and the daughter Bona to the

SIGISMVNDVS I. REX POLONIAE, MAGNVS DVX LI=
TVANIAE, RVSSIAE, PRVSSIAE, MASOVIAE, SAMAGI=
tiæ, & c. Dominus & hæres, belli artibus pacísq; clarus, uictorijs celebris, pietate & religione
insignis, iustus, clemens, benignus: Anno ætatis LXXXI, Regni ueró sui XLI
obijt: Anno à Christo nato M. D. LIIII. Aprilis I. die.

Sigismund I

Dauphin. But Maximillian, the Hapsburg, the overlord of Milan, desired to strengthen his hand in eastern Europe and bethought him of Bona. She was proposed as queen to the widowed king of Poland, Sigismund Stary, meaning Sigismund the Old. She was twenty-four, he fifty-one.

The wedding took place at Naples in the year 1518 with all the pomp and pageantry of the Renaissance. A chronicler gives a minute account of what was worn by every guest. Bona herself had a bodice of brocade, a necklace of dazzling jewels and an intricate braiding of the hair sparkled with golden spangles. Her cousin, Vittoria Colonna, was in attendance. Nothing is told of her save what she had on. The menu was enough to incapacitate the couple for the journey to Poland. Here is a little sample:

> Les pigeons en papillote.
> Le roti ordinaire, avec mirausto, à la sauve au vinaigre.
> Les gateaux florentins.
> Les lapins avec leur sauce.[13]

After fiddling, feasting and dancing the party went by carriage to the coast to travel as far as possible by sea. Isabella took leave of the last of her offspring whom never again would she see.

When Bona was crowned at Cracow she was not the queen of barbarians.[14] Poland had for some time been open to the influences of the Renaissance which she was greatly to foster. Cracow should become a new Milan. Italian architects and artisans, scholars and theologians were gathered into her circle. Italian became the court language. Poland came to be one of the most cultivated countries of Europe. Bona at the same time, like uncle Ludovico, combined cultural efflorescence with statecraft.

In foreign relations Poland should dominate eastern Europe, in part by extending her borders. Prussia became a tributary in 1525 and Lithuania by stages was formally joined with Poland in 1569. Turkey was so much a European power that King Sigismund could address the sultan as *Serenissime ac potentissime princeps, amice et vicine noster carissime,* "Most serene and powerful prince, our dearly dearly beloved friend and neighbor." [15] A treaty of peace was made with Turkey in 1533.

Then too, Bona desired to keep a hold on Italy, north and south. In the north we have noted her connection with Milan. In the south she was the duchess of Bari and granddaughter of the duke of Rossano and lord of Naples. To keep a hold on Milan she would have to stand in with France which had not infrequently made an incursion into Lombardy. To retain a hold in the south required the good graces of Spain and the Hapsburgs, for, although Naples was not ruled from Madrid, her rulers were Spaniards. The favor of the papacy was also requisite, for without it no power survived long in that region. Bona manipulated an unstable balance by an adroit and even devious diplomacy.

Internally she undertook to make Poland a centralized national state in accord with the pattern emerging in Spain, France and England. This meant that she must curb the power of the lords, lay and clerical. One way was by special favors to magnates and bishops. She appointed all of the bishops by express permission from successive popes and with the consent of her husband.[16] As to the qualifications for the bishopric, a bishop himself voiced what was evidently her opinion that the criteria should be "noble birth, capacity to wield authority and devotion to the state and sovereign, and, if private life were not above reproach, the incumbent would serve the state with diligence.[17] Her chancellor said that she would be willing to appoint an atheist, a Porphyrean (Porphyry was an early opponent to Christianity) or a marrano.[18] Opinions differ as to the quality of her choices. Gamrat in his own day was dubbed Bacchus. Yet a modern says that he was maligned. He was in fact a remarkable statesman, dedicated to the consolidation of the royal power and at the same time a patron of arts and letters in which he was himself proficient.[19] These qualities in the age of the Renaissance were, however, not necessarily incompatible.

A further way to strengthen the monarchy was to pit one obstructionist against another. The gentry controlling the diet, could be pitted against the magnates in the senate. The nobility could be set against the episcopacy and this required no effort, seeing that opposition to the clergy was rife among Catholics of undeviating orthodoxy. The nobleman Tarnowski, a devout

Catholic, was vehement in his denunciation of the church. Nor was there any difficulty in arousing opposition to Rome. A correspondent who told Bona she was "the one pillar of religion in the land" adjured her to keep Rome out of it.[20]

She could also abet dissident religious groups, whether simply non-Catholic or anti-Catholic. Poland was in any case the most religiously pluralistic state in Europe.[21] This was partly because the components of the state included groups long since diverse, in the east the Orthodox, Armenian and Tartar Muslim; in the west the Lutheran, following the incorporation of Prussia in 1525. Sigismund was willing to be "the king of sheep and goats." He did think some were goats and tried to keep them out of his pastures by edicts against heresy, which, however, he did not enforce. And the goats did come in. Lutheranism infiltrated from Prussia. Polish students returning from western universities: Wittenberg, Basel, Zürich and Geneva, imported not only Lutheranism but also Calvinism and Zwinglianism. The Italians, swelling the court of Bona, were largely responsible for introducing Antitrinitarianism. Whereas Michael Servetus was burned at the instigation of Calvin in Geneva in 1553 for denial of the Trinity; in Poland the Antitrinitarians enjoyed toleration for some seventy years.

Just where Bona stood on the religious issues is difficult to appraise. Of all the women in these volumes she among them deserves least to be called a woman *of* the Reformation. Her primary interests were political and secular. She may, of course, have thought of herself as God's elect lady to modernize the Polish state. Catholic piety may be inferred from a prayerbook with an exquisite miniature of the nativity brought by her from Italy.[22] But she may have prized it more for the miniature than for the meditations. She did show concern that a Carthusian monastery be adequately staffed,[23] but this may have been because she expected monks to be saints, while bishops might be sinners.

She was certainly not nosing out heresy, for to her confessor, the Franciscan Lismanini, she gave a copy of the sermons of Bernardino Ochino,[24] the one time general of the Capuchins, who in 1542 had defected to Geneva. Which sermons she gave we are not sure. If those published after his "apostasy," they certainly diverged from Rome. If prior, they were at least suffused with that Franciscan lyricism which made the rigidities of Rome un-

A miniature from the prayer book of Queen Bona

palatable. Lismanini is said to have been shaken as to his papal allegiance. More to the point, alike for Bona as well as for him, is that he read without her objection twice a week after dinner to her son, Sigismund Augustus, out of the *Institutes* of John Calvin. Lismanini later became openly a Calvinist.[25] And Bona's physician, Blandrata, became dubious as to the Trinity though he was still a good Catholic at the time when he felt her pulse.

On several occasions she interceded for the Jews [26] and tried to save a professor educated at Wittenberg from the clutches of his bishop. She failed because the area was beyond her jurisdiction.[27] The cynic may find an ulterior motive for her every act, but this at any rate is clear: she did not have the nose of an inquisitor. She was essentially a *politique,* more concerned for the stability of the state than for the victory of a single confession.

One of her qualities drew fire in Poland, rapacity. She had a passion for those treasures, which "moth and rust can corrupt," and they in turn their owners. A Polish poet, Mikołaja Rej, heralded as the father of Polish vernacular literature, included her in his compendium of satirical verse. He would not have dared to fling obvious darts at the queen, but in an encomium there is a thrust. He wrote:

> Bona means good and well named is she.
> Noble her blood and of high degree.
> Brilliant the mind of this eminent dame.
> Heralded now, eternal in fame.
> She came from *Italia,* land of the muse.
> Addicted to finery. This can abuse.
> Reared in her youth in an excellent way.
> Which land she most blessed one cannot quite say.[28]

The sting here is in the word finery. She collected enough jewels to stock a museum. But the gems of nature and the masterpieces of art were by no means the sole objects of her expenditure. She needed immense sums for the dowries of her daughters, the wages of mercenaries, the salaries of craftsmen, the materials for edifices and fortifications, the expenses of ambassadors and the like. She tried to relieve Poland by bringing in the revenues from her Italian estates, but the Italians did not readily allow

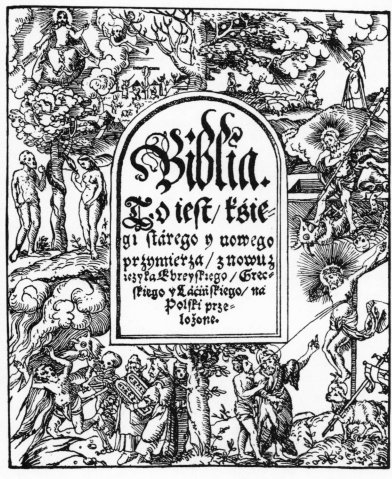

The title page of Budny's translation of the Bible into Polish

their wealth to be exported. In volumes of her correspondence one need only run the eye down the pages to hit the words Naples, Bari or Rossano. She even wrote the Archbishop of Rossano to collect tithes to be applied to her revenues. He answered that for the last thirty years in his diocese the sheep had been so badly shepherded that they would yield no wool. As a churchman he could not use force. Let her confer on him civil jurisdiction.[29]

Complaint is understandable. Nobody loves a taxgatherer. All in all she gave Poland a sound administration, notably when, as her husband failed, she became the real ruler.[30] A modern biographer rates highly her achievement:

> Bona exerted a powerful influence on the form of the modern Polish state not only by reason of her intellectual gifts but even more because she possessed a profound feeling for the essential needs of the state. She fused completely the foreign Italian strand with the emerging Polish national movement. In the social and economic sphere she aspired through her excellent reforms to create a strong authority based on a just distribution of goods. In many respects Bona was ahead of her times and that was the tragedy of her life.[31]

Such is a modern judgment, but the tragedy was rather that she was not sufficiently ahead of her times to let a son marry for love. She was shattered to learn that Sigismund Augustus, having lost the wife whom he had dutifully married at her behest, had now become enamored of an exquisitely beautiful Lithuanian princess, Barbara Radziwill, and in the presence of her brothers had been secretly married without the consent of his mother, his sisters or the Polish diet.[32] Bona stormed, raved and raged. Had she not dismissed the charming gallant to marry the pudgy old king of Poland? To be sure, she had become fond of him afterwards and in his last illness had given him the care of a nurse and a maid,[33] but in marrying him she had conformed to the wishes of her mother. And now, this son of hers, the only son, the beloved son, for whose training she had so sedulously cared, totally unmindful of his duty to his mother and the state, had yielded to infatuation with a lovely face! Bona had planned to have him married to Anne of Ferrara, daughter of the Duke and his wife Renée (see our first volume), herself the daughter of a former king of France. Such a union would forge a link again with northern Italy and even more with France, which could then be induced to bring pressure on the Sultan to restore Bona's daughter to the throne of Hungary.[34] And now this mad son had wrecked it all!

Why did he do it? Is a romantic infatuation sufficient to explain the flouting of his mother and stultifying of the ethos of his age? A possible additional factor is the influence of Erasmus and Calvin. Erasmus enjoyed a great vogue in Cracow in the forties and some half dozen of his books were in the library of Sigismund. Erasmus was scornful of political marriages. "Princes," said he, "should eschew foreign alliances and especially marriages beyond their borders. What sense is there in an arrangement whereby a marriage suddenly turns an Irishman into a ruler of the Indies or makes a Syrian into a king of Italy? Actually royal marriages do not insure peace. England made a matrimonial alliance with Scotland and James of Scotland nevertheless invaded England." [35] As for Calvin, whom Sigismund had read under the tutelage of Lismanini, the Genevan council at Calvin's instance ruled that if parents refused consent to children of age they might be overruled and compelled to pay a dowry.[36] Sigismund may have been not only enamored but also impelled by conscience.

The news of the marriage came out at the time of the death of the old king, whom the son, already elected, now succeeded. The monarchy in Poland was elective, though the election usually adhered to the dynastic principle. Bona's son was now Sigismund II. The Polish diet was as much outraged as she that the king should marry a girl so far beneath his station. Her brothers were dukes in Lithuania, not kings. And even had she been the daughter or sister of a king, the Poles did not want a Lithuanian. Her brothers might then become too powerful in the Polish diet. Nationalism was at stake. Apparently not religion. Barbara was a good Catholic who during the ferment that followed, went daily to Mass for comfort. Her brother was a Calvinist, who harbored even those with Antitrinitarian leanings. There was no prospect that she would either persecute heretics or secede from Rome.

SIGIS···  ·  AVGVSTVS, DEI GRATIA REX POLO-
NIAE, MAG. ·S DVX LITVANIAE, RVSSIAE, PRVS-
SIAE, POMERANIAE, SAMAGITIAE AC MAZO-
VIAE, ETC. DOMINVS ET HAERES. ·
ANNO DOMINI        AETATIS
M.D.LIIII.            XXXV.

Sigismund Augustus

The diet held clamorous sessions. Sigismund sat through them quietly. Some demanded that he repudiate the secret marriage. He replied that the diet should no more demand of him that he

Barbara Radziwill

break his word to his wife than to the diet. Then, it was said, let him abdicate. A compromise was suggested. He should be king. He should keep his wife but she should not be his queen. He referred the proposal to her brothers and they would have none of it. He informed the diet that on no point would he yield. The leader of the opposition capitulated, "overcome by the king's patience and constancy." Barbara was crowned.[37]

Bona and her daughter Sofia refused to attend the coronation. Thereafter Barbara's health speedily declined. Her hope had been that she might live just long enough for the coronation. Bona softened. Lismanini shuttled from son to mother to effect a reconciliation. Bona at length commissioned him to appear before the court with letters from herself and her daughter, which he read in Latin to the assembly: [38]

> Her most sacred and serene, royal Highness [Bona], by the grace of God queen of Poland, my most gracious mistress, after long and mature deliberation, seeing that what has happened is the will of the Most High, because whatever happens is by His will and pleasure, and also because this is the will of his most sacred Majesty, her beloved son, which should not be contravened, wills that your sacred Majesty [Barbara] should be his spouse, his queen and the partner of his bed, therefore her sacred Majesty [Bona] promises to acknowledge and honor your serene Highness [Barbara] as her daughter and beloved daughter-in-law and has deigned to commission me her servant [Lismanini] to bear witness this day to her conscience. She prays and hopes that the Lord God will speedily relieve you [Barbara] of your present illness and restore you to your pristine health.

Barbara replied through her minister, "Yes, if only it please the most gracious Dispenser." [39]

She lived but shortly thereafter. As her disease progressed the stench was so great that the physicians could not bear to stay long in the room, but Sigismund held her hand to the end. Her brothers desired that she be interred at Cracow along with the queens of Poland, but she said, "Ungrateful Poland shall not have my bones." [40] Burial was at Wilna, the capital of Lithuania.

Sigismund followed the cortege largely on foot all the way from Cracow. Two years later, at the behest of the diet, he submitted to a political marriage in the hope of supplying an heir. When he died, twenty-one years after her death, his last word was "Barbara." [41]

Some have claimed that the coronation made Poland Catholic.[42] The Protestant clergy were not willing to officiate and the Catholics took over. Sigismund rewarded them by edicts against heresy which he did not enforce. But the Protestant objection to Barbara was not that she was Catholic, but that she was Lithuanian. "Precisely," comments this historian, "Nationalism destroyed religion." The verdict is too simple. Sigismund could never have broken with Rome unless he had been able with Martin Luther to say, "Let goods and kindred go. This mortal life also." He was not so minded. The inheritance of Bari, Rossano, and Naples, was worth a Mass. Besides a sharp break with the Catholic Hapsburgs might open a flank to the Turks.

For Bona the coronation was decisive. Barbara she could recognize. Sigismund she could hardly forgive. Back she would go to Italy. The decision arose not simply from frustration over an obstreperous son, but also from despondency because of the failure of her attempt to convert Poland into a consolidated national state under a strong monarchy. The government was moving instead in the direction of an autocratic oligarchy.[43] Whether any one could have succeeded in diverting the trend is open to question. In Germany the territorial states did indeed achieve internal consolidation, but not a national unity. That process was not completed until the twentieth century and in Italy not until the nineteenth.

Bona had several counts against her. She was a woman. Of course a woman could exert a powerful influence. Witness Isabella in Spain and Elizabeth in England. But Bona was resented in Poland, when as the old king grew enfeebled, she usurped authority, not only from him but also from the nobles.[44] The Polish aristocracy might have been more maleable under a man. A further count was that she was not Polish. Isabella was Castillian and Elizabeth an English Tudor. Italianism was, to be sure, for a period very much the vogue in Cracow. At the same time many Poles resented the Italians and especially one reared in the atmosphere of the political intrigue characteristic of the despots of the Italian Renaissance, where a sudden death aroused suspicion of poison. That inference was made in the case of the early death of Bona's father and now she was suspected of having poisoned Barbara. Added to all this was her manner. Tomicki, her most faithful chancellor, confided to a complainer that the queen was imperious, blustering and badgering.[45] Sometimes she was brutal. When a blind archbishop stood in her way she told him she wished he had lost not only his eyes but his tongue.[46] Her yoke chafed.

The reason alleged for leaving was health. Poland had no hot baths and the Italian climate suited her better. Sigismund and the diet were aghast. The departure of a queen of thirty years would reflect on the land. Was she not beguiled by nostalgia for the glamor of a vanished youth? Would she be happy there? She would miss the honors accorded her in Poland.

"Honors accorded me in Poland," she sniffed. "My mother was honored at Bari and I would be."

"Oh, yes," answered the diet, "but remember, if you go you will no longer be the Queen Dowager of Poland, though, if you return, your status may be renewed."

She answered that if her health improved she might come back.

Sigismund strove mightily to detain her. "This business of her health is just a ruse," he told the diet. "She wants to get back to Italy just to get her hands on all the properties of Bari, Rossano and Naples and to cut me off from my rightful inheritance from my grandmother. She should not be permitted to leave. If there is no other way, though it would grieve me greatly, she must be imprisoned. It would be a genteel incarceration." The diet thought constraint unseemly. Bona delayed long enough to see Sofia married to the Duke of Brunswick. To be sure, he was only a duke, but then she was only a daughter.[47]

After the wedding Bona started out. Lest she be detained on the way, she had obtained safe conducts from Philip of Spain and his wife, Mary Tudor, and even more important, from the emperor. Bona is alleged to have traveled with twenty-six carriages, each with a span of six horses, so great was the heap of

Queen Bona widowed

jewels accumulated over the years. The tapestries she had to leave behind. At Venice she received an ovation and Pavia gave her a pageant with the sort of triumphal arch that had entranced her youth.

The reception in the south was far different. No one wished her to come in person to collect the revenues never sent. And before long, Philip of Spain, having won a resounding victory over the French, was so impoverished by the expenses of the war that he simply appropriated all of Bona's holdings, leaving her nothing. Death quickly followed. Not even a nurse or a maid attended her. Only her confessor wiped her lips. Her body was placed in a wooden box and moved to the church to stand between two candles, unattended. As they burned down, the box caught fire. Her charred remains were interred in the lovely chapel. A bronze table was installed at the expense of Sigismund.[48]

After some years Spain repented of the shameful confiscation and restored the inheritance to the heirs only to breed between them and their mates strife and bitterness. The heirs by then were only three: Sofia the Duchess of Braunschweig, Anna to be the queen of Poland and Katherine, the queen of Sweden. To her we shall return after further examples from Poland.

## NOTES

1. Pociecha, Władysław, *Królowa Bona*, 4 vols. (Poznan, 1949). The fullest and best documented biography. The same author has a brief article on her in the *Polski Słownik Biograficzny*. Kosman, Marceli, *Królowa Bona* (Warsaw, 1971). Popular and not documented.

2. Colison-Morley, L., The Story of the Sforzas (London, 1933).

3. *Ibid.*, pp. 146-7.

4. Beatillo, Antonia, *Historia di Bari* (Naples, 1637), reprinted in *Historiae Urbium et Regionum Italiae Rariores* III (Bologna, 1965) p. 175.

5. Nulli, Siro Attilio, *Ludovico le Moro* (Paris, 1922), p. 98.

6. Ratti, Nicola, *Della Famiglia Sforza*, 2 vol. (Rome, 1794). Vol. II, *Donne illustri di Casa Sforza*, p. 63.

7. Dina, Achille, "Isabella d'Aragona Duchessa di Milano e di Bari," *Archivio Storico Lombardi*, Ser. V, No. 48 (1921), pp. 269-457. Croce, Benedetto, "La Spagna nella Vita Italiana Durante la Rinascenza," *Scritti di Storia Letteratura e Politica* VIII.

8. Sannazaro, Jacobo, *De Partu Virginis*. The Yale Beinecke library has an edition of 1526.

9. *Della Vera Tranqvillita dell'Animo* Con Privilegio Paul III, Aldine

Press, Venice 1544. Copy in the Beinecke Library of Yale University. This tract has been attributed to Bona's mother. So by Pociecha in the encyclopedia article (note 1 above). But Ratti (note 6 above) shows that the author was another Isabella Sforza, the natural daughter of Giovanni Pesaro. She was born in 1503 (p. 172). Pociecha gives a Spanish title, *La Quietud del alma*. Did it ever so appear?

10. Dina (note 7 above), p. 451.

11. Ratti (note 6 above), p. 73.
    Beatillo (note 3 above), p. 189.

12. Croce (note 7 above), pp. 130ff. The story was told in the form of a novel with fictitious names. A contemporary identifies Belisena as Bona.

13. Giacomo Salvatore, "Bona Sforza à Naples, 1505-17," *Gazette des Beaux Arts* III, 18, Nov. 1897, pp. 409-22, and III, 19, May 1898, pp. 393-406.

14. *The Cambridge History of Poland* (Cambridge, England, 1950). The general background and Bona's aspirations.

15. *Acta Tomiciana* XIII, No. 203 and XIV, No. 228, p. 360.

16. *Ibid.*, No. 68 and Pociecha (note 1 above), II, 385.

17. *Acta Historica Res Gestae Poloniae Illustrantia* I (Kraków, 1878) p. 15.

18. Pociecha, II, 386.

19. Kosman (note 1 above), p. 9.

20. *Acta Tomiciana* XI, Nos. 183 and 268.

21. Tazbir, Janusz, *A State without Stakes*, Kosciuszko Foundation, Library of Polish Studies III, 1973.

22. For a reproduction see p. 142 in this volume.

23. *Acta Historica* (note 17 above), No. 81.

24. Lubienszki, Stanislas, *Historia Reformationis Polonicae* (Freistadt, 1685), p. 18. Copy in the Beinecke Library of Yale University.

25. *Ibid.*, p. 41, and Bukowski, X. Julian, *Dzieje Reformacyi w Polsce* (Kraków, 1883), 1, p. 346, quoting Węgierski, *Slav. Ref.* p. 126: Wotschke, Theodor, "Francesco Lismanini," *Zeitschrift für die Provinz Posen* XVIII (1903), p. 219; Hein, Lorenz, *Italienische Protestanten und ihr Einfluss . . . in Polen . . .* (Leiden, 1974), pp. 32, 35.

26. *Acta Tomiciana* XVI, No. 53 and Zivier, *Neuere Geschichte Polens* (1915).

27. Kot, Stanislas, *La Réforme dans le Grand Duché de Lithuanie* (Brussels, 1953), p. 10.

28. Rej, Mikołaja, *Różnę Peztnadki Swiata Tego* (Warsaw, 1953), p. 112.

29. *Acta Tomiciana* XIV, No. 416.

30. *Acta Historica* (above note 17), XIV, p. 198.

31. Kosman (note 1 above), p. 9.

32. Biographies of Barbara: Szajnocha, Karol, *Barbara Radziwiłłówna*

(Biblioteczka Uniwersytetow Ludowych, Kraków, n.d.). Nowakowski, Tadeusz, *Die Radziwills* (München, 1967). Neither of these studies is documented. There is a sketch with bibliography by Pociecha in the PSB (note 1 above).

33. Kromer, Marcin, *Martini Cromeri De Origine et Rebus Gestis Polonorum Libri XXX* (Basel, Oporinus, 1555), p. 686. Copy in the Beinecke Library of Yale University. The statement occurs in Kromer's funeral oration for Sigismund I, and is reproduced in Sabastiano Ciampi, *Notizie . . . colle Vite di Bona Sforza . . .* (Firenze, 1833) p. 36.

34. Pociecha, "Poselstwo Andrzeja Jakubowskiego . . ." *Odrodzenie i Reformacja w Polsce* V (1960), p. 107.

35. *Erasmi Opera* (Leiden), IV, 637B and 602E. For the works of Erasmus in the libraries of Sigismund and Kmity including the *Institutio Principis Christiani* see Universitas Jagellonica, *Acta Scientarum Litterarumque,* Schedae Historicae Fasc. XXXIII (Kraków, 1971), *Erasmiana Cracoviensis,* pp. 35, 48 and 49.

36. *Calvini Opera* Xa, 105-106.

37. *Acta Hist.* (note 17 above), I, No. 835.

38. The text is given in Latin in Balinski, Michala, *Pisma Historycne* (Warsaw, 1843), 1, p. 208. Her death wish on p. 181. A Polish translation is given with Latin interspersed and textual variants from Balinski's in Przezdziecki, Aleksander, *Jagielloniki Polskie XVI wieku* (Kraków, 1868), 1, p. 263 (abbr. Jag.).

39. Szajnocha (note 31 above), p. 76.

40. Jag. (note 38 above), I, p. 267.

41. Jag. I, pp. 265, 268 and Nowakowski (note 32 above), p. 62ff.

42. Wotschke, Theodor, "Kirchengeschichte Polens," *Studien zur Kultur und Geschichte der Reformation* 1 (1911).

43. Lepzy, K., "Zur Frage der Zentralization und Soveränität Polens im 16. Jahrhundert," *La Renaissance et la Reformation en Pologne et en Hongrie* (Budapest, 1963), pp. 415-23.

44. *Acta Tomiciana* XIV, p. 198.

45. *Ibid.,* XVII, No. 218, p. 306.

46. Jag. II, p. 353.

47. See Szajnocha (note 31 above).

48. The sequel is described by Klemens Kantecki, *Die Neapolitanischen Summen* (Posen, 1882). Brief biographies of the 180 Italians variously employed in the court of Bona Sforza are given by Danuta Quirini-Popławska, "Działalnosc Włochów w Polsce w i Połowie XVI Wieku . . ." *Polska Akademia Nauk—Oddział w Krakowie Prace Komisji Nauk Historycznych* N2.32. (1973).
R. A. Borth, a Pole long resident in Scotland, informs me that Docent St. Cynarski is about to publish new documentary material on Bona's last days.

# Katherine Weigel

From the queen for whom politics meant life we turn to one for whom religion brought death. She was the first martyr among the very few to suffer for religion in the Poland of the sixteenth century. Katherine Zalaszowska was the wife of Melchior Weigel, a nobleman, a goldsmith and a member of the Cracow council. The Lutherans claimed her as their martyr because she objected to the elevation of the host and the Antitrinitarians because she rejected the doctrine of the Trinity. Her judges condemned her for Judaizing and they were probably right. The Jews in that period were influencing the Christians, some of whom shifted their Sabbath to Saturday. Her arguments against the Trinity were those of the Jews and for that matter of the Moslems, who objected that human begetting cannot be attributed to God, whereas the Christian Antitrinitarians took their departure from the doctrine of the two natures in Christ, divine and human. If he propitiated God in the divine nature God would be propitiating God, but if in the human nature the Son would be subordinate to the Father.

With regard to her we have only the records of two trials. Here are excerpts translated from the Polish in turn translated from the Latin of the ecclesiastical records:

In the year 1530 on Friday the fifth of July Katherine Melcherowa, the wife of Melchior Weigel, a citizen and city councilor at Cracow, suspected of the errors of the Jewish religion, having failed to meet the deadline of a deposition of her confession as to the articles of the Catholic Church, was subject to a judgment of default. In spite of this she was allowed to appear before the present court, meeting at the quarters of the bishop and consisting of Mikołay Bidlenski, scholastic and Vicar Spiritual, Jakop Arciszewski, the Official General, Jerszt Myskowski, O.P., Doctor. They interrogated her as to the reason for her non-appearance at the designated time. She replied that it was not out of contempt but she had become suddenly involved and did not find suitable occasion. They inquired then as to the articles of the faith of the Apostles and the entire confession of the Catholic Church, all her rites and usages decreed by the Holy Ghost: the absolution of sins, the salvation of the soul as an undoubted conviction. She admitted that she had had certain doubts as to the faith arising from feminine curiosity or rather mental derangement and softening of the brain, but now she had no longer any doubts and begged forgiveness for her error, imploring for herself the mercy of Holy Mother Church, who does not shut the door on the penitent, but in mercy receives him. The comissars ruled that the said Melcherowa should recant in some church in Cracow, or in the aula of the bishop in accord with the order that she renounce and recant all the errors of the Jewish faith and all of the suspicions which have given rise to great scandal.

In the year 1530 on Thursday the 11th of August, pursuant to the sentence on the above-mentioned Melcherowa, she was brought to the quarters of the bishop to make public recantation of the errors of which she was accused. Failing to comply, she was committed to prison. Some time later she was brought before a company of ecclesiastics to make her recantation. They examined her again on the articles of the faith, the teaching of the Roman Church. She must renounce adherence to any sect and the errors of the Jewish faith of which she was accused. Kneeling, she then placed her hand upon the gospel and invoked a curse upon herself should she fail, and she swore submission to the canons. The bishop then accepted her return to the bosom of Mother Church and bestowed his blessing, admonishing her never again to fall into the like errors and at the same time enjoining upon her readiness to receive instruction in all of the canons and like features.

Evidently she did not regard a coerced vow as binding, for nine years later we find her again on trial. The secretary of the court gave this account:

In the year 1539 Melcherowa of the city of Cracow, a white-haired woman of eighty years, because of adherence to the Jewish faith, was burned in the marketplace of Krakow, as I have witnessed. Assembled at the palace of the Bishop Gamrat were all the canons of Cracow and the collegiants to hear her confession of faith. She was examined with respect to the creed. Did she believe in God the Father Almighty, the maker of heaven and earth? Yes, she did, and added that he is the creator of all things visible and invisible, whose mind and providence are unfathomable. We are his people and all things are his according to the spirit. She rambled on at length extolling the power of God and his inexpressible providence.

Then again she was interrogated: "Did she believe in Jesus Christ His only Son, our Lord, who was conceived by the Holy Ghost, etc.?"

She replied, "God never had a wife or a son, nor could he. For him there is no need of sons who die, since the Lord God is eternal. He cannot be born and he cannot die. We are his sons and all are sons who walk in his appointed way."

Here the collegiants cried out, "Be done with it. You're wrong, you wretch! The prophets have testified that the Lord God, according to the spirit, sent his Son to be crucified for our sins that his obedience might atone for our disobedience from the days of our father Adam."

Then the doctors labored with her greatly. But against all their persuasions she remained adamant that God could not be a man and could not beget. When she could not be dissuaded from her Jewish religion she was pronounced guilty of blasphemy against God and was turned over to the temporal arm (meaning the secular court, because the ecclesiastical court could not pronounce the sentence of death). A few days later, as above mentioned, she was sent to the stake. She went to her death unaffrighted.

Another source adds, "as if to her wedding." Gamrat, who presided at her condemnation, was that lecherous and bibulous bishop nicknamed "Bacchus."

## BIBLIOGRAPHY

Excerpts from the acts of her trial are given in Polish translation by Julian Bukowski, *Dzieje Reformacyi w Polsce*, I (Kraków, 1883), pp. 176-9. A condensed version is given in Lukasz Gornicki, *Dzieje w Koronie Polskiei*, ed. Henryk (Wrocław, 1950), pp. 12-13. Professor W. Urban informs me that the originals of the sources utilized by Bukowski have been lost. Other contemporary documents are extant and Professor Urban has kindly sent me extracts from the Latin acts *Archiwum Kurii Metropolitalnej w Krakowie, Acta Episcopalia* 16 fol. 124v-125v; 130r-131v; 134v-135r; 18 fol, 88v-92 and 31r. This material adds nothing save for more vilification of "apostasy and Jewish perfidy" and the jargon of jurists who, to cover every contingency, must use six synonyms. The sentence reads, "We teach, say, decree, pronounce, define and declare that . . ." The statement that she went "as to her wedding" is in Adrian Węgierski, *Systema Historico-Chronologicum Ecclesiarum Slavonicarum* (Rhenum, 1672), p. 207. Yale University Library, collection of 1742, number 8.6.19. The Polish version of a year earlier has been reprinted: Woiciecha Węgierskiego, *Kronika Zboru Ewangelickiego Krakowskiego* (1671). Reprint Roku, 1817, pp. 3-4. Copy at the Pacific Unitarian School for the Ministry, Berkeley, Calif.

# Jadwige Gnoinskiej

Jadwige Gnoinskiej made a significant contribution to the religious and cultural life of Poland for which she has received only the most minimal recognition. She sparked the foundation of a "new Jerusalem" which became a veritable city with a distinguished academy and an extensive publishing house.[1] She was the wife of a Polish nobleman, Jan Sienienski, Castellan of Zarnov, in the days of Sigismund Augustus. The husband was a Calvinist, the wife an Arian. This was the name applied to those who like the ancient heretic Arius subordinated Christ the Son to God the Father. The group was called also Antitrinitarian and later Unitarian. The adherents preferred to be called simply Brethren, or more precisely Polish Brethren to distinguish them from the Czech Brethren.

Jadwige brought her husband from Calvinism to this persuasion. This may have been more of an achievement than to found a city, for at the instigation of Calvin, Servetus the Antitrinitarian, had been burned at Geneva. Having achieved the conversion, Jadwige induced her husband to place at the disposal of the Arians a sufficient portion of his vast estate for the founding of a utopian community. The recognition accorded to her memory was the naming of the city from the heraldic device on her coat of arms, a red crab on a field of white. In Polish the word for crab is *rak*. The possessive adjective is *rakow*. This was the form used for the name, *Rakow,* the City of the Crab.[2] In the

subsequent annals she does not appear, though her husband and son are mentioned. In 1638 the husband was described as venerable at the age of seventy. In that case he must have been only nineteen when he made the donation in 1567.

Examples of the rak (crab or crayfish) on the heraldic device of Jadwige Gnoinskiej

Her intentions can best be inferred from the deed of donation.[3] The terms were exceedingly generous. The settlers were to be exempt from all the imposts and obligations commonly levied on tenants and serfs. They were to have free use of the surrounding woods, rivers and meadows. Each house should have a sufficient allotment for a garden and meadow, though cattle might also range on common meadows. The inhabitants were to keep in repair bridges, walls and moats and for the purpose might use cakes of dried manure. The rights were guaranteed in perpetuity.

More significant than such benefits was the assurance of inviolable religious liberty. Each should be free to follow the leading of the spirit. Such a proviso, if taken to the letter, would have admitted Muslims and Jews, not to mention Lutherans and Calvinists. But this was certainly not the intent. Rakow was to be the Zion of the Polish Brethren and there was a hint that the

patron would exercise a measure of control over anarchistic factionalism.

Besides the assurance of livelihood and liberty was the attrac-
tiveness of the area;[4] the soil somewhat sandy to be sure, but
adequately fertile, the climate temperate and salubrious, the site
entrancing with woods, streams and a lake in a land smiling with
luxuriant meadows. Settlers came from near and far, dug wells,
felled trees and built houses standing to this day. Life was sustained from the produce of the soil and crafts. A visitor felt himself transported to a world remote from wars and tumult where
men were so modest of behavior as to seem angels, though spir-
ited in debate.[5]

In all of this description we find no word of the patroness. Had
she perhaps passed early from the scene? That may well have
been the case. There is, however, another explanation, plausible
though not demonstrable, that the neglect of her memory was a
phase in the disintegration of a utopia. At the outset the Racovians patterned their New Zion on what they conceived to have
been the model of the early church, marked by communism,
pacifism, egalitarianism, laicism and feminism. In the course of
less than half a century these features were eroded.[6]

The communism appears to have been rather of the sharing
of surplus than the common ownership of all property, rather
the type mentioned in Acts 5:4 than in Acts 2:44-45. Some nobles
indeed arrived penniless. Others retained their estates and lived
on them rather than migrating to Rakow, yet were in close touch
with the Racovians. This lack of uniformity may well have contributed to the breakdown. Another factor was disillusionment
with respect to the religious communism of the Hutterian Brethren in Moravia. A visit left the impression that their regime was
too rigid and authoritarian. Basically the circumstances were
different. The Hutterians were exiles living in enclaves isolated
from their hosts, whereas the Racovians were Poles living among
Poles and subject to the pressures for conformity.

Pacifism at first required total abstention from warfare. The
brethren who sat in the Polish diet wore only wooden swords.
But this stance was hard to maintain in a country at war with
the Tartars. The first stage in accommodation was the acceptance

of noncombatant service and the final stage a complete acqui-
esence.

Egalitarianism required that master and man, mistress and
maid should call each other brother and sister. Ideally there
should be no serfs and there were cases of emancipation but this
appears never to have been the rule.

Laicism meant that in the earliest years there were no official
ministers. Every member was a mouthpiece of the Holy Ghost.
But when all the mouthpieces began to fulminate against each
other the factionalism became so rife that some members left and
those who remained reinstated the ministry.[7]

Finally there was feminism,[8] the most important item for this
study. But before we can discuss disintegration we must inquire
whether there was anything to disintegrate. Is it true that the
sisters enjoyed an equality with the brethren even to the point
of preaching? The testimony comes almost entirely from hostile
sources and one may be inclined to dismiss the stories as the fab-
rications of malicious slander. To this the reply is that the
charges were not sufficiently malicious to have been simply
slander. The standard slander against dissident groups in the
history of the church has been that of sexual orgies. In the re-
proaches leveled against the Brethren an erotic slant was slight.
It was entirely absent in the earliest instance of the allegation of
female preaching. The witness is none other than the Queen
Bona Sforza herself. Just before her departure for Italy (1551)
she had a conversation with Cardinal Hosius who tells us that
when he lamented the spread of heresy into every corner of the
land, she added, "Yes, every crucifix in Cracow has been smashed
. . . and even women, I hear, are preaching. While my husband
was alive I would have taught them what it is to preach. I'm a
Christian queen and I won't stand for any of this nonsense." [9]
Who were these women? Calvinists might well have demolished
the crucifixes but neither they nor any other main line Protestants would have allowed women to preach. With whom are we
left if not the Polish Brethren?

Twenty-two years later, in 1573, an abbot named Reszka testified to the predominant role of women among the Brethren.[10]
"They ware unstable, flitting like Salome from opinion to opin-

ion," thus showing that Protestantism ends in anarchy. Finally in 1614 we have the charge, leveled by a Jesuit, that among these "spirituals" a minister may be required to give heed to the commonest folk, a tailor, an artisan, a peasant and a woman.[11]

Thus far we have encountered no Oedepodian banquets, nor do we ever, but there were two instances in which sex was involved. The first was a charge by that same Abbot Reszka [12] levelled against Ochino, whom we met in our first volume when he was the Savonarola of his generation in Italy. Since then, having turned Protestant, he had incurred successive banishments until in 1564 he landed in Poland. Now Reszka asserted that Ochino had written a work dedicated to King Sigismund Augustus in defense of polygamy. The subject was touchy at the moment because the king was in the plight of Henry VIII. As his third wife, King Sigismund had married the sister of Barbara, his first wife. No one of the three had given an heir. This was regarded as a judgment of God for disobedience to the Mosaic prohibition of marriage with a deceased wife's sister. Should Sigismund then take a bigamous wife? [13] Ochino, continued the allegation, had openly from the pulpit in Cracow defended this course till he was shouted down by the clamor of women and forced to leave the country.

There are two errors here. He had indeed written on polygamy in a work dedicated to Sigismund. The tract was a dialog in which the arguments in favor of polygamy were advanced by one party and refuted by the other. The conclusion was that polygamy might not be allowed except by reason of a special revelation, such as that given to the patriarchs of the Old Testament. Secondly, Ochino was not banished for this. The king wished to expel radical Protestants. The Catholics said this would be tacitly to tolerate other varieties. The king then banished foreign Protestants and among them Ochino.[14]

The most significant point for us in all this is to know who the women were. Since Ochino had been excommunicated by Rome, his hearers would not have been Catholics. And since he had been banished from Zürich and Basel they would not have been Zwinglian, Calvinist or Lutheran. Whom, then, have we left if not the Polish Brethren? Two points here are significant:

one that the objectors were protesting against any hint of polygamy; the second that women dared to shout down a preacher.

The next instance is the tale that a minister of the Brethren, after a wedding, exhibited the bridal pair standing in a garden beneath a tree, stark naked.[15] The minister denied the allegation, but the rumor may have been true somewhere and the incident not erotic. The pair were Adam and Eve and this dramatization was parallel to that practised by men of Rakow who constructed heavy crosses and under their weight staggered about the land in fulfillment of Christ's injunction to take up the cross.[16] These Racovians were living in a perpetual Oberammergau, dramatizing both the Old Testament and the New.

This then is the testimony of the hostile sources. There is one confirmation from within the group. We have a letter reporting on the first synod of the Brethren held in 1565 before ever Rakow was founded. This letter twice declares that the decisions of the synod had the approval of the brethren and the *sisters*.[17] Yet in 1614 an apologist of the Brethren, replying to the Jesuit above quoted, answered that a tailor might indeed be endowed with the spirit but in the deliberations of the church no heed was given to the opinions of boys and *women*.[18]

Why in the course of fifty years should there be in the annals no mention of the role of women and at the end a flat denial? The suggestion has already been made that the change was a phase of the disintegration of a utopia. Then why did the utopia disintegrate? For two reasons: the absence of persecution from without and the lack of isolationism from within. The Brethren, as we have noted, were tolerated in Poland for a hundred years and shared in the common life. They were laughed at by friendly neighbors and ridicule from within is often harder to bear than vilification from without. Their young did not relish being jeered for wearing "lousy sheepskins," [19] nor to see cartoons of one of their ministers as a fox in clerical garb proclaiming the teachings of Mohammed on the Trinity. Because preaching by women was even easier to ridicule it may have been the first feature of the utopia to go and the least to be remembered. Do we have here an explanation of why Jadwige Gnoinskiej was accorded not so much as an epitaph?

One should, however, add that after another half century female ministry was revived. When, during the Swedish invasion of 1655-60, the men were in the army, the women took over in the affairs of the church. Katarzyna Potocka is recorded to have

ARRIANI &
vera Mohometanorů
Evangellorů minc-

SOCINIANI
progenies pallio
strorum tecti

Caricature of an Arian (Socinian)

engaged alike in pastoral care and also preaching.[20] Her activity can have lasted scarcely more than three years because in 1658 the Arians as a whole were banished. The reason for her assumption of ministerial functions was obviously the absence of men, but even so would she have been so presumptuous had there not been a latent tradition of equality? In any case during those turbulent years there was little time or inclination to delve into archives that credit might be given to the woman who initiated the new Jerusalem and Jadwige is still remembered only as the Lady of the Crab.

## NOTES

1. On the influence of Rakow see the essays by Tazbir and Tworek in Lech Szczucki, *Wokół Dziejow Tradycji Arianizmu* (Warsaw, 1971).

2. Stanislas Lubienski, *Historia Reformationis Polonicae* (1585), p. 239. Copy in the Beinecke Library of Yale University.

3. The documents on the founding are given in Polish in Stanislas Tworek, "Raków Ośrodkiem Radykalizmu Arianskiego, 1569-72" in *Raków Ognisko Arianizmu*, ed. Stanislawa Cyrarskiego (Kraków, 1968).

4. Lubienski, note 2 above.

5. E. Morse Wilbur, *A History of Unitarianism*, vol. I (Cambridge, Mass.), p. 361 and note.

6. Stanislas Kot, *Socianism in Poland* (Boston, 1957) on the general disintegration. On the Racovians and the serfs see Wacław Urban, *Chłopi Wobec Reformacij w Małopsce w Drugiej Połowie XVI W.* (Kraków, 1959).

7. On factionalism: Lubienski, "Poloneutychia," in *Humanizm i Reformacja*, ed. Chrzanowski and Kot (Warsaw, 1927), p. 423.

8. On the role of women: Wacław Sobieski, "Modlitewnik arjanki," *Reformacja w Polsce* 1 (1921). Aleksander Brückner, *Roznowiercy polscy* Ser. 1 (Warsaw, 1905), pp. 132, 148, 196-200, 273. Stanislas Kot, *Le Mouvement Antitrinitaire au XVIe et au XVIIe Siècle* (Liege, 1936), p. 81.

9. *Hosii Epistolae* II, nr. 1559 for the year 1556.

10. Reszka's letter in Jan Czubek, *Pisma politycnzne z czasów pierwsego bezkrólewia* (Kraków, 1906), Nr. LVI.

11. Smiglecki, *Refutatio vanae dissolutionis Nodi Gordii* (Kraków, 1614). p. 67. Cited in Sobieski (note 8 above), p. 59, note 5.

12. Reszka, *De Atheismis et Phalarismis Evangelicorum Libri Duo*, Stanislao Rescio Presbytero (Neapoli, 1596), p. 59.

13. Zygmunt Wdowiszewski, *Genealogia Jagiellonów* (1968), pp. 106-8.
14. Roland H. Bainton, *Bernardino Ochino* (Florence, 1940), p. 133 ff.
15. Lubienski (note 2 above), p. 197.
16. J. Paleolgus *Defensio Verae sententiae de magistratu politico* (Losk, 1580), pp. 315-19. Text supplied to me by W. Urban.
17. George Hunston Williams, *The Radical Reformation* (Philadelphia, 1962), pp. 688 and 699.
18. Smalc (or Smalz) *Notae in libellum M. Smiglecii* (Kraków, 1614); p. 33, cited by Sobieskie (note 8 above), p. 59, note 6.
19. Kot, p. 61.
20. Jan Dürr-Durski, *Arianie polscy* (Warsaw, 1948), p. 17. There is some material about her in the sketch of her husband by Jan Czubek, *"Wacław z Potoka Potocki," Archiwum do Dziejow Literatury i Oswiaty w Polsce* VIII, 1895.

# Three Polish Poets

There was one area in which women in all lands had a recognized role, namely in devotional literature: poems, hymns, prayers and meditations. They did not write treatises on systematic theology. Perhaps they were not interested. Perhaps they acquiesced in the prevalent low esteem of their competence. With respect to the devotional they were unchallenged. We have noticed in the earlier volumes the meditations of Katherine Zell in Germany, the religious poetry of Vittoria Colonna and Olympia Morata in Italy, the verses of Marguerite of Navarre in France and the meditations of Katherine Parr in England. In Poland the Protestant movement gave rise to a considerable production of this genre whether by women or by men in order to meet the need for household instruction in prayer and song. Witness the accompanying woodcuts. Of the three women about to be noticed here the first was Calvinist, the other two Arian.

ZOFIA OLESNICKA, the Calvinist, was related either as sister or wife to Mikolaj Olesnicki, the lord of Pinczow, who turned over an abandoned cloiser church in that city to the Calvinists and authorized the removal of all the images. In this church was celebrated in the year of 1550 the first evangelical Lord's Supper. We know very little about Zofia beyond these bare facts. We do have her picture. And we have the hymn because of which she is called the first poet in the Polish tongue. The hymn was published in 1556 with a four-part musical setting. Notice that

Zofia Olesnicka

each of the parts was printed separately, marked discant, tenor, alto and bass. The form of the hymn was that of the acrostic very popular in that period. The first letters of each line reading down give the name of the author. In this case I am quite unable to carry over the device into English because twice she has used the letter Z, for which the only possible words in our tongue are zeal and Zion. Zeal might do but Zion never. Here is a free rendering:

> With gladness of heart, Lord, I praise Thee.
> Thy mercy has deigned to behold me,

And turned not away from Thy servant
Who trusts herself wholly to Thee.

Thou hast hidden in secret Thy kingdom
From the eyes of the wise and the prudent,
Because they trust to their reason,
As our dear Lord has told us.

Thou hast called us Thy little children
And shown Thy measureless mercy.

Family prayers and hymn singing in Poland

Musical setting to her hymn

We have, therefore, reason abundant
To sing every hour of Thy glory.

O fount of love everlasting,
Uphold in the power of Thy spirit,
That in Thy truth we be constant
And faithfully keep Thy commandments.

Better to safeguard Thy treasure,
Which neither moth nor rust can corrupt
Than enmeshed in the ways of the world
To forfeit Thy favor forever.

In this, Lord of heaven, sustain us,
For vain else is all our endeavor,
Be we not drawn by Thy love
And fainting upheld by Thy spirit.

We falter not in assurance
That Thy promises shall be kept to Thy servants.
What Thou deignest to give in Thy pleasure
We trust to receive without measure.

Let each, then, with seemly rejoicing
Praise with his soul the Lord's goodness.
For He will work for us wonders
While foul maggots receive not forgiveness.

Sing then to the Lord of all goodness.
Sing ye faithful. Sing of His glory.
Soon by His grace He will save us
Through the merit and death of His Son.[1]

Our second Protestant poet was an Arian, who died slightly before the founding of Rakow. Her name was REGINA FILIPOWSKA, the wife of the prominent Arian minister alleged to have dramatized the scene of Adam and Eve in the garden. She was married to him between 1550 and 1552 and was very active with him in the Arian movement until her death in childbirth in 1559. Her hymn is dated 1558. I have been able to discover the text of only the first line: "My hand to Thee, Almighty God." [2]

The third example is another Arian poetess of the period after the Racovians had circumscribed the role of women. The date of her prayer book can be determined only approximately. There is a reference to an event of the year 1621. A single copy has been preserved in the British Museum. The acrostic discloses her name as MARGARETA RUAROWNA, or undeclined Margaret Ruar. Her father was Marcin Ruar, a very distinguished leader among the Arians. In this instance the acrostic can be carried over into English because she does not use the letter Z. Here is a slightly free translation:

M ighty is prayer to close the sluices of heaven.
A nswer gives prayer to all of our needs.
R iches exceeding and wealth without measure
G od has conserved, safe in His keeping.
A bundant for flesh, abundant for spirit.
R adiant joy and resolute courage.
E lijah prayed once for the closing of heaven.
T hen he implored that the heaven be opened.
A lways to pleading God gives a prompt answer.
R ain from the cisterns descended in torrents.
U ntil then the earth parched now yielded abundance.
A lready the ground had been hardened and arid
R eturning the dew moistened the furrows.
O how needful is prayer who can question
W hat is so potent, so powerful and active?
N owhere receive we else blessing eternal.
A ll is of Thee. Of ourselves we are nothing.

The prayers themselves disclose a fervent devotion to Poland, the more so perhaps because the Ruar family had been transplanted from Germany and may, therefore, have been eager to display undivided loyalty to the new fatherland. Here are a few excerpts from the prayers.

"O King, all the nations are as a drop from the bucket and are accounted as dust in the scales. The nations in Thy sight are as nothing and are esteemed as vain and empty. The whole

world before Thee is as the quivering of the balance, as the drop
of the morning dew when it lights upon the earth. All the
peoples are under Thy sway. Thy chastisement is upon other
nations. One after another is broken, as vessel upon vessel. One
Thou raiseth up and one casteth down. Empires are born, grow,
flourish and wax old and still unripe are by Thy holy will consumed."

"Protect, O Lord, Thy kingdom of Poland. Thou wert her
defender when shortly ago in her ordeal, the Turks at Thy behest withdrew (in 1621). How can we assume that this was due
only to the courage and valor of our people or to chance when
the sequel, as a clarion, proclaims the work of Thy hand? As our
nation owes to Thee her deliverance, so ought we to render unto
Thee thanks unceasing and far in excess. Thy munificent boun-
ties display beyond cavil the knowledge of Thy truth."

"Chasten not Thy people because of those who assist not in
dispelling errors, but rather for the sake of Thy children among
them extend Thy mercy. Deliver not Thy people to the shame
and mockery of other nations. Save us from dissension within,
from the bloody sword of the enemy and from the cruel oppres-
sion of the pagans."

"Give unto us peace under Thy fatherly hand. Forfend contention and confusion within our borders. Restrain the envy of
neighbors that Thy children, O Lord, may dwell in Thy kingdom in righteousness and peace. Establish the kingdom of our
fathers. Grant us Thy protection as of yore. For Thy mercy's
sake pardon our transgressions. Suffer us not to succumb to dis-
ruption but do good unto Thy children among whom hitherto
Thy glory has found an abode." [3]

## NOTES

1. The text is given in modern script in *Historya Literatury Polskiej* VI (Kraków, 1844), p. 446. The musical setting is in Wojcicki, K.W.T., *Biblioteka starozytnych pisarzy polskich* I. wyd. 2 (Warsaw, 1859), pp. 9-16.
2. There is a brief biography of her in PSB VI. A biographical notice of her poem is in Szweykowski, Zygmunt M., *Z dziejów polskiej kultury muzycznej* (1958), p. 290. No. 14. This poem also is an acrostic.
3. The text is given in Sobieski, Wacław, "Modlitewnik arjanski," *Reformacja w Polsce* 1 (1921).

# _Anna_ _Marchocka_ _Teresa_

Anna Marchocka [1] is included here as a representative of the Catholic Counter-Reformation. Her name as a religious was Teresa in recognition of Teresa of Avila. That Anna should turn to Spain is indicative of the foreign influences playing upon Poland in this period. Protestantism and notably radical Protestantism, was sparked and fanned extensively by religious refugees from Italy.[2] One thinks of Lismanini, the Calvinist, Vergerio, the Lutheran, but more particularly of Blandrata, Alciati, Stancaro, Ochino and the Sozzini among the radicals. The Counter-Reformation was spearheaded by two Spanish movements; that of the Jesuits, founded by the Spaniard Ignatius Loyola, and the Carmelites, reformed largely through the efforts of Teresa of Avila.[3]

Her autobiography was published in Polish translation in 1608. Following her lead, Anna Marchocka wrote an autobiography, the first of its kind to be composed by a woman in Poland. There is a great similarity in their careers. Anna, like Teresa, was plagued by both physical infirmities and spiritual depressions. The historians of mysticism inquire which influenced the other. A novice like me can only observe that physical weakness can alter a disposition and an emotional crisis may bring about a physical collapse or, on the other hand, a rejuvenation.

Teresa (Marchocka) tells us that, reared in a devout family, she considered becoming a nun, but deferred decision like Augustine, whose saying she quotes, "O Lord make me chaste, but not yet." She felt unworthy to take the vows and constantly bemoaned her deficiencies. After such hesitation she entered the order of the Carmelites, who had already been introduced into Warsaw from Belgium. During the ceremony of induction the rule of St. Francis was read. She was eager to conform and was appalled to discover that the rigors of the rule were in abeyance. At that point Joseph appeared to her in a vision. One recalls the devotion of Teresa of Avila to Joseph. He now berated Anna and the whole convent for the utterly shameful disobedience to the injunctions of the founder. Anna was so upset as to fall into an illness which endangered her life. On recovery she set about the work of reform. Two new Carmelite houses were erected at her instance. One was at Cracow. Apparently her efforts were not so bedogged as those of Teresa in Spain.

The autobiography of Anna oscillates, like that of Teresa, between aridity and the overflowing of the fountain of mercy and the glory of God. The style is jerky and disjointed, betraying intense emotion. She delineates five stages in her religious experience. In the *first stage* the soul suffers from dryness, with inability to understand, feel or imagine. It is beset with alienation from God and from man, overpowered by fear, dread and estrangement. The mind is feeble, the memory faint. Forgetfulness is such that one knows not where one is, whether awake or asleep. The lapse may be no longer than the saying of an *Ave Maria,* but seems interminable. The mind races in frantic uneasiness and can light on nothing, can press nothing out of the wine-press, as it were. God is locked out.

The *second stage* is even more dramatic. The spirit is weighed down, grievously wounded, finding everything bitter, distracted by diffidence in which there is still some hope, and desperation in which there is none. The will is impotent. This is the suffering of hell.

The *third stage* brings alleviation. The mysteries are still unraveled, but God no longer hides himself in thick darkness, is not walled by fear and distance. One has the certitude that God is within oneself. The experience is incomprehensible, indescribable. There is an antinomy between the feeling of forsakenness and the craving for God engendered by the sense of God within. Reason finds these two hard to reconcile. "I was troubled," she says, "till I read the reflections of Holy Mother (Teresa) in the sixth book of the *Castles (Moradas)* and the second chapter. Everything she there writes I have experienced. By this reading I became enlightened and tranquil."

In the *fourth stage,* the God in man completely takes over. Everything now disappears, all ideas, all knowledge, all means and ways. There is a sort of nothingness, yet at the same time a great desire, wish and affection for the Lord. This is not, however, an abiding state. There is a constant rhythm. Again the spirit is disquieted, the body breathless. The spirit is forsaken like Christ's upon the cross, and the body is like his in the deposition. One does not then desire human company, dislikes being asked, "What has happened? Why are you groaning?" One must retire, be alone. How can one speak of the supernatural with the light of heart? "I turned again," she says, "to the writing of the Holy Mother in the last section of the sixth book of the *Castles* but I would not yield my pride and allow her to help me. My confessor chided my stupidity in not hearkening to her word and enjoying the divine gift."

In the *fifth stage* the soul stands naked before God. There is nothing but a feeling of an abyss of pain, of tears before the Lord, such as Christ experienced on the cross. This cannot be expressed by the pen unable to write in tears. What a comfort then there is when the load is lifted and one is made free by commitment to the will of the Lord. One is now content with everything without any striving to understand what is better, what more truthful, with no desire of any good for oneself, with no fear of evil, no yearning for heaven, no dread of hell, no will, intelligence and understanding, but with full freedom of the divine will. This is all I feel, nothing more, nothing from me, everything from the Lord. Nothing remains for the soul but to believe and trust in God, without any knowledge, without any understanding, nakedly.

The alleviation of her agonized cry, "Oh that I knew where I might find Him!" was the experience of ecstasy, occurring sometimes as often as thirty times in a year. Her editor says that the

unusual feature of her narratives is that with dispassionate ob-
jectivity she describes the physical accompaniments. Once her
hands became cold, the heart thumped, she was as if in a fever
and yet felt no cold. Another time her hands became numb especially on the left and the left eye was affected. Breathing was
hard. Everything went black. Slowly she regained her senses. The
sisters at the Carmelite monastery at Cracow thought she was
suffering from epilepsy and so did the doctor. She was distressed
that such experiences set her off from others who did not understand. If only they could see what she saw. When the experience
was joyful she had the sense of jumping and flying, when painful she felt like a batter of bread in the oven when the yeast
rises and the crust explodes.

Here is a prayer which voices her aspirations:

> Oh my Father, Thou knowest, Oh Lord, my desire and I
> know that neither thought, nor word, nor imagination can
> attain. I beseech Thee, Oh merciful God, grant unto me
> light and learning that I write not that which is not worthy
> to be written. Let me not be subject to passing fancy, nor to
> the base and vile, the empty, futile and worthless. Suffer me
> not to sink in the slough of doom. O glorious God! deliver
> me from distrust and affliction. Be Thou to me a physician
> and buoy that my words may have purpose and profit. Grant
> me to be blessed forever. Humbly I beseech Thee, my Father.
> Cover me with Thy pinions, enlighten mine eyes that I wan-
> der not in a haze, knowing not what to write nor where.
> Let me but know Thee, Oh God." [4]

## BIBLIOGRAPHICAL NOTES

1. There is a sketch of her in the *Polski Slownik Biograficzny*, XIX under the name *Marchocka, Anna Maria*.
An analysis of her mysticism is given by Karol Górski, *Od religynosci
do Mystyki* (Lublin, 1962), pp. 108-21.
He gives a critical edition of her autobiography as "Autobiographia
Mystica M. Théresiae A Jesu Carm. Discalc (Anna Maria Marchocka),
1603-1652." *Scriptores Poloniae Ascetico-Mystici* vol. II (Poznan,
1939).

2. On the Italian influence on Polish Protestantism, Massimo Firpo, "Sui movimenti ereticali in Italia e in Polonia nei secoli XVI-XVII" *Revista Storia Italiana* LXXXVI, Fasc. II, 1974.

3. The Spanish influence is covered by Stefanna Ciesielska Borkowska, "Mystycyzm Hispanski na Gruncie Polskim" (Kraków 1939) *Polska Akademia Umiejetnosci Rozprawy Wydzialu Filologicznego.*

4. *Autobiographia,* p. 112.

I am indebted to Professor Alexander Schenker, head of the Slavic department at Yale, for help in reading Anna's sixteenth century Polish.

Katarina Jagellonica

# SWEDEN

## *Katarina Jagellonica*

Katarina, the queen of John III of Sweden, may seem an odd choice to illustrate the role of women in the religious movements of Sweden in the sixteenth century. She was not Swedish, but half Polish and half Italian, the daughter of Sigismund I of Poland and his wife Bona Sforza of Italy, to whom a sketch has already been devoted. But Katarina had a greater influence in Sweden and beyond than any other woman of the period. Sweden at that time was no isolated outpost of Europe but was in intimate relation with the lands of the north, England and Denmark on one side, Poland and Russia on the other and with the whole Mediterranean world. A volume of documents from the reign of Katarina and John, edited in a modern edition, is in seven languages. Of these the queen spoke at least five and probably all. She had Polish from her father, Italian from her mother, Latin from her humanist education, Swedish from her subjects, German from diplomats and craftsmen at her court, French and Spanish from the royal envoys. She conversed with her husband in German or Italian, since she did not know Finnish nor he Polish. The court language was Italian.[1]

John's marriage with Katarina precipitated them both into dire trouble. The hereditary principle governed the succession, and on the death of Gustavus Vasa the crown went to his eldest son by a first marriage, Erik XIV. There were three half brothers by a second marriage. Magnus died mad. The Vasas were bril-

liant but unstable. John and Karl were made dukes, the former
in Finland, the latter in Södermanland. They were largely independent but nevertheless feudatories of Erik, the king. This ambiguous relationship made trouble for John. Without his sovereign's consent he wooed and won the Polish princess, Katarina
and gave to her brother, Sigismund II, a huge loan, taking for-
tresses in pledge. The ensuing events are related in an anonymous
tract so dramatic as to suggest fiction, were not the author Marcin
Kromer,[2] a Pole loyal to his country and to Rome and desirous
of strengthening Poland against Russia through a union with
Sweden. Protestantism should be exterminated in both lands.
The best means would be to effect the union under a sovereign,
a scion of both the Vasas and the Jagellons, and firm in the
Catholic faith. There was only one who could fulfill the condi-
tions. Sigismund, the son of John of Sweden and Katarina of
Poland and reared in her faith. To prepare the public mind a
piteous tale is related of the sufferings and steadfastness of the
child's parents.

Kromer tells us how John, the duke of Finland, was enamored
of the Polish princess, renowned for her beauty and sought after
by the Russians and Italians alike. John gave as partial dowry a
huge loan to the Polish king with castles in pledge. The wedding
was celebrated in Poland with all of the accustomed festivities.
Erik did not attend. The journey of the bridal pair to Finland
was arduous and protracted. The ship, which tried to take them
from Riga, was ice bound. A channel was cut, allowing a return
to Riga where they were detained for forty Sundays, waiting for
clement weather. On the next trip the ship was taken over by the
Swedes and the passengers set ashore. They had to walk thirty
miles. When they did reach Finland there was no welcoming
delegation and but one sled for the conveyance of the queen
alone. When the news spread five hundred horsemen appeared
and carried the pair to the royal quarters to be dined and wined
and feted with dances.

Not for long! Erik accused his brother of treason for having
made an independent treaty with a foreign power, and for having withheld taxes from the royal exchequer. All Finns were
released from the oath of fealty to the duke. Eight thousand

Swedish soldiers came to take John and Katarina to Sweden. John sallied from a castle with only a few hundred retainers and repulsed the attackers. [This sounds like an Old Testament miracle, unless perhaps the Swedes were loath to join in this fratricidal strife.] Then came a ship a-sailing. John thought it brought help from Poland. It was from Sweden. He capitulated and on St. Bartholomew's day in 1563 he and Katarina were conveyed to Sweden. Erik told her that since her husband was guilty of *lèse majesté* the marriage bond was dissolved. If she would leave him she would be free. If not, she would share his captivity. She responded by holding up her wedding ring on which were engraved in Latin the words, "Whom God hath joined together," and vowed again to God to be faithful "till death do us part."

They were for a time marooned on an island with no protection save a little shelter made from sails, then were transferred to meager quarters in the castle of Gripsholm. Visits from friends were forbidden, but merchants smuggled in money in wine bottles. [Presumably this was also the method of introducing letters from her sister Anna in Poland of which we know from other sources.] In captivity Katarina gave birth to Isabella. For swaddling clothes she purchased a few rags from attendants. The child lived only a year and a half. Next came Sigismund, the great consolation of his mother. Katarina was at length allowed as attendants one or two Polish women and as chaplain a somewhat enfeebled old Polish prelate.

John, in the meantime, besought his brother to bring him to trial that he might vindicate his innocence. He was transferred to Stockholm to appear before the king. A mile from the city, guards forced him to take a road lined with gallows on which were hanging his former servants. Then came a squabble over jurisdiction. Erik insisted that the case should be heard by the archbishop or by the Riksdag (the council). John said that he was amenable only to the king. Erik then ruled that, since he would not plead before those delegated, he should be relegated to more severe imprisonment. Katarina, in the meantime, was sick with suspense.

For her a more grievous ordeal was in store. Ivan the Terrible, the Czar of Russia, sent word to Erik that the Polish princess,

Katarina, should be given to him as wife. The czar sent one hundred sable hides, lynx furs, costly jewels, while promising 500,000 gold pieces and 30,000 knights to augment the king's armies in addition to castles in Livland. Erik pondered this proposal five times. The czar informed him that if he declined Russia would attack not only Livland, but Sweden as well. Erik well knew that the move would be unpopular at home, executed seven nobles and then sent word to the czar to come for the lady. Ivan sent 500 horsemen with sleds to the border to await her coming. Erik then assured Katarina that by consenting she would cement the friendship of the two countries and earn for herself an eternal weight of glory. Let her tell the czar that she alone had desired to be the czarina of so mighty a lord. Erik himself would conduct her and would be to her as a father and none would give her more friendly counsel.

Katarina gave a flat no and appealed to God. Erik was minded to kill John and ship her off, but she was pregnant (as it turned out with Anna to be named for her aunt in Poland). John besought his brother to wait at least until after the birth of the child. The Riksdag let Erik know that such unchristian behavior was not to be tolerated. One of the nobles delivered a protest. Erik had him killed. Then Erik's son remonstrated with his father, "You do wrong, O king, to kill an innocent lord without trial. I'd rather be killed than to be guilty of such cruelty." And he was then killed by his father's hand. Another nobleman upbraided him, "My Lord King, why have you murdered these two? You have killed the heir apparent. If you murder your noblemen you too will fall." Erik screamed, "You have forbidden me to send the princess to Moscow. You're a traitor," and cut him down.

The next day there appeared before Erik a man in white raiment, saying, "Tyrant you have nurtured the plan to kill your brother and send his wife to Moscow. As God's mouthpiece I tell you that his anger is kindled against you. If you do not permit your brother and his wife to return to his kingdom, God will take away your kingdom and will deprive you of your reason. You will tear off your clothes. You will eat grass like an ox, and as a beast you will wander among the crags of the forest. God will send you into everlasting imprisonment at the hands of your enemy. He has heard the cries of your brother and his wife. He will take them under his mantel and you will be consigned to everlasting damnation."

Erik asked his attendants if any one had entered the room. They assured him there had been no one. Then he sent a hench-man with retainers to kill John and Sigismund and to send Katarina to Moscow. The soldiers, informed of their mission, re-fused. Erik's one time teacher, a man of eighty years, came to remonstrate. He was cut down. Erik then, observing the disaf-fection of his people, suddenly veered, and summoning some of them said, "Who is your king?" "You, my Lord," was the re-sponse. "I am not your king," he answered. "I am a tyrant. Sweden has never had such a tyrant." Stripping himself of his clothes he went out into the woods. After three days and nights he was found and brought back to Stockholm. Three nobles were chosen to carry on the administration. Restored to his senses, Erik asked how he came to be in this plight. When told, he recalled the vision of the man in white raiment.

Erik then composed a humble supplication to the mighty Prince John who should be the king of Sweden and Finland and to the Princess Katarina, to be the queen of Sweden, beseeching them out of Christian charity to forgive his offenses. He would make over the crown, the scepter and the robe to his brother and his heirs and would be to them a faithful subject. All the jewels and gold in his treasure chest were to be made over to John and Katarina. Erik would like to have a little bit of terri-tory left to him as a feudatory of his brother, who, he hoped, would spread the unadulterated Word of God and hearken to the teachings of Luther and Melanchthon. Erik begged to be allowed to write his memoirs without abusiveness. When he should be gone let none besmirch his memory and let a marble monument commemorate his achievements.

John refused to accept the abdication, swore fealty to his brother as king and asked only to be restored to Finland. The half brothers met. At first John did not recognize Erik, then doffed his hat. Erik in turn genuflected, asking pardon in the name of God. Gladly would he resign and let John take over the kingdom. With the sign of the cross he besought forgiveness from Katarina. Then he held out his hand to young Sigismund, who slapped it. Erik laughed and kissed the boy. The banquet was delayed by a contest of humility between Erik and John, each insisting that the other take the higher place.

Then came war with Denmark. John raised a considerable force to support his brother. The Swedes, thereupon, greeted John with acclaim saying, as it were, "Saul has killed his thousands, David his ten thousands." Erik was consumed with jealousy. He had under way a great banquet to celebrate his marriage to his concubine, a commoner, whom the Riksdag had at last given him permission to make his wife and queen. Erik now conceived a plan at the banquet to murder John, Sigismund, the other brother Karl and all the nobles in attendance. Now the mother of John and Karl happened to be friendly with the mistress whom Erik was about to marry. This girl got an inkling of the plot and dropped a hint to the mother who relayed it to her sons. They promptly raised troops and took over the castle. Erik continued preparations for the banquet. When the food arrived without the guests he went out to inquire, only to find himself beleaguered by his brothers. After a brief resistance he capitulated, and was consigned to a prison where he spent his remaining years studying mathematics and astronomy. Kromer concludes, "He wrote an illustrated history of his war with his brother. [What became of it?] He was very fat. This is the worst history of our century. The Christian was more cruel than the Turk."

Erik had spoken of the great treasure he would confer upon John and Katarina. John could not find it and excavated unavailingly around the castle of Stockholm. He thought of having Erik tortured to disclose the spot. Katarina stopped that. Many plots centered around Erik to rethrone after dethroning John. The Riksdag decreed that if there were another conspiracy Erik's life would be forfeit. There was another of which he may have been quite unaware, seeing that he was closely guarded. The jailer was ordered to make away with him. Poison was used. That is authentic. A modern exhumation has disclosed arsenic. John may not have signed the death warrant but he did not intervene to save him. Erik's son then fled to the continent where he was supported in part by funds supplied by Katarina.[3]

On John's accession to the throne Katarina's period of influence began. Like her mother she was a devotee of the Italian Renaissance to which John also was addicted. He was the most learned of all the kings of Sweden and in addition to command of the languages already mentioned was able in Greek to read St. Cyril. He had, besides, a passion for building. Just as Bona Sforza, the queen's mother, had made of Cracow a new Florence, so Katarina and her husband wafted *bellissima Italia* to the land of the midnight sun. Imported architects and artisans left the imprint of Italian design on the public buildings of Sweden with colonnades and gardens.[4] Witness this sketch of the portion of the castle at Stockholm reconstructed during her reigns. Unfortunately the garden and swimming pool do not appear.

But our concern is not with Katarina as a princess of the Renaissance but rather as an agent of the Counter-Reformation. She was a Catholic, but not of the type then regnant, which sent to the stake those mildly deviant from the standards of the Council of Trent. Her Catholicism was of the same stripe as her mother's, stemming from the liberal circle of Naples in the early years of the century. In the fifteen seventies a Catholic of Katarina's stripe was an anachronism. Sweden was Lutheran but also not of the rigid type which had developed since Luther. In Sweden there were at the same time some remnants of Romanism as well as leanings to Calvinism and Philipism, named for Philip Melanchthon. Nevertheless, by the time Katarina became queen, one is able to say that Sweden had become "morbidly susceptible to any whiff of popery." [5]

We must now double back to give a brief review of the stages of the Reformation in Sweden up to this point. John's father, Gustavus Vasa, having thrown off the lordship of Denmark, had established a national church in Sweden in 1523, a decade before a like development in England. He might have been ready to recognize a titular headship of the pope provided the king were "the highest protector of the Holy Christian faith throughout the whole realm," with authority to appoint bishops, collect

J then natt tå han förrådder wardt/toogh Jesus brödhet/tacka dhe Gud/brööt/ och gaff Läriunganar och sade / Tager/äter/thet ta är min lekamen/som för ider ythgiffuen warder/ Thet görer til mijn åminnelse.

Sammalunda toog han ock kalken/ sedhan Natwarden hållen war/tacka dhe Gudh/gaff them och sadhe/Dricker här aff alle/ty thetta är min blod/ som är thes nyia Testamentzens/hwilken för mongom ythgutin warder/til syn

Communion in Both Kinds in 1548
From the *Handbook*

tithes and expropriate church property. Rome would make no such concessions and Sweden became independent.

The reforms were at first comparatively mild. The Mass became a communion, not a sacrifice and was said in the vernacular. The cup was given to the laity (communion in both kinds). There were to be no private masses said by the priest alone for the dead. Marriage was allowed to the clergy. Some popular practices, at first optional came to be forbidden: the use of images, pilgrimages, invocation of saints and the use of incense. Holy days were reduced. Tithes were collected by the government. For a time there was some overlapping of old and new. The *Handbook* of 1548 shows the administration of the cup to a lay woman, but the priests are still in Roman vestments. By 1552 one could say that "the Roman Church had ceased to exist in Sweden."

The Lutheran Church which succeeded was, however, not simply a state church. Gustavus said that his appointees in the highest sees were no more inclined to implement his entire program than "a Frisian cow to spin milk." When Olavus Petri and another of the chief reformers were insubordinate, the king accused them of treason and condemned them to death. Popular feeling forced commutation to fines. When the Emperor Charles V in 1549 tried to impose the *Interim,* which conceded to the Protestants only communion in both kinds and recognition of clerical marriages already contracted, the entire Swedish clergy declared themselves ready to die rather than submit. By the end of the reign of Gustavus in 1560 the point had been reached when the crown would have tottered had the king either tried to return to Rome or to impose his own will unconditionally.[6]

Under Erik XIV, despite his temporary insanity, the reform became more Lutheran. One little episode is illustrative. Giving the wine in the eucharist to the laity heavily drained the Swedish liquor supply all of which had to be imported. The Calvinists were willing to substitute cherry juice. The Lutherans objected that Christ did not say, "This is my blood," with reference to cherry juice. Erik defused the controversy by opening the royal wine cellars to liturgical use and thereby eliminated any Calvinist substitute.[7]

This brings us to the period of John and Katarina. Her Catholicism, though mild, was nonetheless genuine and she did desire to bring Sweden back to Roman obedience. So did John. But why John? A Protestant historian, writing early in the next century, said that he had succumbed simply to the pressures of his wife, "for, as Ambrose says in his thirty third epistle, 'No temptation is equal to woman.' "[8] But John did have convictions of his own. During his captivity he had read not only the Church Fathers but also the near contemporary George Cassander.[9] He was a German Catholic bishop very active in the forties and fifties in attempts to heal the breach between the confessions. The Lutherans and the Calvinists, said he, are not heretics. The true Church includes Catholics who are penitent for their sins and Protestants motivated only by a sincere concern for reform. They are agreed on the essential points necessary to be believed for salvation. The essentials are the doctrine of justification by faith and the observance of the sacraments. As to the Mass, Cassander rejected the doctrine of transubstantiation, held that the Mass is not a sacrifice and is of no benefit in and of itself *(ex opere operato)* regardless of the attitude of the recipient. Over nonessentials the unity of the church ought not to be broken. Within the church, wide diversity should be allowed. In the interpretation of Scripture, tradition should be revered. By implication the popes and councils were not infallible. Since no pope of that day would have sanctioned reforms along these lines, the initiative, said Cassander, would have to be taken by princes. To this role John was not disinclined. Cassander exerted considerable influence. The Augsburg *Interim* of 1549 was justified on the ground that it was asking from the Protestants acquiescence only as to the non-essentials. Melanchthon cheerlessly subscribed and the influence of Melanchthon in Sweden was high.

Another factor to influence John's mind was the pattern of the Anglican Church. While still the Duke of Finland and not yet at odds with his brother, he had been sent by Erik to England to negotiate a marriage for him with Queen Elizabeth. Nothing, obviously came of that, but John did there observe a church independent of Rome, retaining much of the Roman liturgy and some of the vestments and firmly under the control of the crown. This

The Augsburg Confession in Swedish in 1566 with the Swedish coat of arms and a dedication to the Princess Elizabeth, King John's sister

system would be ideal for Sweden and it would not of necessity require a break from Rome so long as the pope was simply the spiritual head of Christendom.

John's artistic tastes may well have been of influence. He was entranced by the music of the liturgy [10] and perhaps in his subconscious there may have been a lingering feeling that outside of the Church of Rome there is no salvation, for he is alleged once to have said that he would give all of his toes to get his father out of the hell to which he had been consigned for having expelled the Catholic Church from Sweden.[11] But this point is not to be pressed. He would have needed several feetfull of toes to cover all of his avowed desires.

Whatever may have been his convictions there were certainly ulterior considerations prompting his willingness to bring his country back to papal obedience. His wife's mother, Bona Sforza, the queen of Poland, had immense properties in Italy at Bari, Rossano and around Naples.[12] All of this she willed in equal proportions to her three daughters: Anna to become the queen of Poland, Katarina the queen of Sweden, and Sofia the Duchess of Braunschweig. The portion allotted to Katarina was sufficient to pay off the entire Swedish national debt. John was out to get it, but he knew very well that he would never succeed if the pope were opposed, because the pope exercised an overlordship over Naples. The actual rulership of the area was in the hands of Philip of Spain and he, too, would not suffer such sums to pass into the hands of a heretic. John's only hope lay in exerting himself to the uttermost to bring Sweden back to Roman obedience.

John had leverage which counted heavily with Pope Gregory XIII in the realm of his cherished political objectives. One was a crusade against the Turks, and, since Venice had made a treaty of peace with them, the only other to whom to look was Philip of Spain. The second objective was to dethrone Elizabeth and replace her with Mary Stuart. Gregory XIII was the pope who excommunicated Elizabeth and released her Catholic subjects from their oaths of allegiance. And the only one, again, who could implement this program was Philip of Spain. He did indeed try later on with the Armada. But at the time he could move neither to the east nor the west because his forces were tied down in the Netherlands.

Now John of Sweden happened to have at his disposal a good fleet, built up by his brother Erik and no longer needed after the peace with Denmark. John had tried unsuccessfully to market the fleet when coincidentally came two bids. The one was from Queen Elizabeth and William of Orange in order to drive Philip and the Spaniards out of the Netherlands. The other was from Philip in order to crush William and neutralize Elizabeth. The pope wanted the fleet to go to Philip. "Very well," said John in effect. "Let me have my wife's Neapolitan legacy and you may have my fleet" (with suitable payment.) But how could the pope, without the most brazen inconsistency, exert himself to transmit such a sum to the wife of a heretic?

How then was Sweden to be purged of heresy? The key was Katarina. She had yielded sufficiently to her husband to take communion in both kinds. Her sister Anna in Poland remonstrated and begged her not to do the like again. Katarina justified herself to Cardinal Hosius on the plea that she had the approval of her confessor who had told her that she could not go far wrong in taking the wine because Christ gave it to the apostles. She knew that this was contrary to the present rules of the church and asked absolution for her disobedience but at the same time begged a dispensation which would allow her to do it again. Would the cardinal by refusal wish "to sow perpetual discord" between her and her husband who had forbidden her to take communion in one kind only?

The cardinal replied [13] that "by no means did he mean to sow discord but one must obey God rather than man and did not Christ say, that whoever loves father or mother (he didn't say husband) more than me is not worthy of me?' Of course you must love and obey your husband and do everything conducive to the conjugal bond but when religion is involved Christ is to be loved and the divine Majesty obeyed, in comparison with which every human majesty is but dust and ashes. Your confessor was mistaken in saying that for you to take the wine was no offense since Christ gave it to the apostles. The apostles were not laymen. And note that when Christ supped with the disciples at Emmaus he broke only the bread. When I translated your letter into Latin and read it to his Holiness he was overjoyed that the lost sheep is returning to the fold and most readily conceded the absolution which you crave but when you asked a dispensation to do it again he was simply aghast. I exhort you, I plead with you, I beg you, don't ever ask this again. As for perpetual discord with your husband I would remind you of the words of Christ, 'I came not to bring peace but a sword.' I will say nothing harsher. Your husband may eventually come around.

"In the meantime talk to him in this manner: 'My king, my lord, my husband, of all mortals most dear to me, I am flesh of your flesh and bone of your bone. You have authority over my body and I would count it a small loss to lay it down for the salvation of your soul. I hope I shall not be an Eve whose persuasion beguiled Adam and brought innumerable calamities upon us all and may you not be to me that serpent through whom Eve was beguiled and deceived her husband. You say it is no sin to take communion in both elements. I agree heartily. In the past it has been allowed but it must be done in accord with the order and observance of the Church. I will readily comply with your demand that I take the cup if only I can do so without disobedience to the Church. Most happily I will comply if you will just listen to one little request of mine. The subjects under your rule have cast out the religion in which I was brought up. I beg you little by little to restore that from which your father seceded fifty years ago. Flee to the apostolic seat of Rome. Ask forgiveness and restoration. Then, since the Church is most clement and indulgent, I am sure that communion in both kinds will be granted, if this concession will minister to the saving of so many souls. For what the Church objects to is not the cup but schism. Let the unity of the body of Christ be restored. Then I am sure this point can be negotiated. If you talk this way to your husband I am confident you will prevail upon him.'"

She did prevail to the extent that John acceded to the introduction of some Jesuits in a new college but with the stipulation that they must operate as clandestine Lutherans. Their successes were not inconsiderable. One was with the young Prince Sigismund. After midnight Mass in the chapel at Westeras where the queen communed through bread alone, the priest secreted a consecrated wafer in his vestment and then drew the young Prince Sigismund into a separate room where Katarina had converted a table into an altar. The priest heard the lad's confession and granted absolution and then asked him whether, having been reconciled to God by a salutary penance, he did not desire a closer union with the divine Majesty through the sacred body of our Lord Jesus Christ. Sigismund with sighs expressed his fervent desire. "Now," asked the priest, "what would you say if the Divine Goodness had resolved at this very moment to prepare this heavenly food for you?" Seeing the awesome silent response the priest fell upon his knees and in a voice choked with tears exclaimed, "See, see the Holy Sacrament which the inexhaustible goodness of God presents to you this day." The boy broke into tears. When he was somewhat calmed the priest continued. "Since you are about to receive this inestimable grace you must engage in return to uphold the Catholic faith and you must promise me, as if I were God, that you will never receive communion in both elements from the hands of heretical priests." The boy swore and communed.

John himself made his private submission to the Church of Rome,[14] but when it came to the restoration of Roman Catholicism in Sweden his invariable reply was that Sweden could never be restored to Roman obedience unless the pope would concede the marriage of the clergy, communion in both kinds and the Mass in the vernacular. The pope replied that even if these points were conceded there was a more serious difficulty. Not a single priest in Sweden was qualified to administer the sacraments, because they were not ordained by those in the apostolic succession. Consequently the only sacrament which could be administered in Sweden was baptism which is valid even if performed by a woman or a heretic. But absolution through penance, the Mass, marriage, extreme unction and even Christian burial were invalid.[15] John replied that the Swedish Church could apply to the Greeks, whom Rome recognized as in the succession. The answer was that the Greeks did not believe that the Holy Spirit proceeded from the Son as well as from the Father.[16]

As for the concessions which John said were absolutely imperative if Sweden could be induced to return to obedience, the pope's constant response was, "Submit and we may negotiate." And John's reply was, "Concede and we may submit." The interchanges dragged on for years. Katarina wished that she might return to Poland but resolved to stand by her post.[17]

But John did go as far as he dared with a revision of the liturgy in a form closer to the Roman. Assembling the clergy he addressed them himself, pointing to "the lamentable divisions among the Protestants by which even their own leaders are so disillusioned that they have been approaching the Greeks. The proper solution is to return to the apostolic, catholic beliefs and practices of the primitive Church as set forth in the Old and New Testaments, confirmed by the infallible testimonies of the Holy Fathers and sealed by their blood. See how far the Swedish liturgy has departed from the ancient models. Compare it with the liturgies of St. James, St. Basil, St. Chrysostom, Saint Ambrose and Saint Gregory the Great.[18] We need to restore the ancient hymns and antiphons, the ancient order of the epistles and gospels during Lent, the cult of the saints, the prayers preceding the preface at the consecration, prayers for the dead, the invocation of the saints, the teaching of the corporeal presence, confirmation, auricular confession, clerical celibacy, extreme unction and the reestablishment of converts." [19]

The most stalwart of the Swedish clergy refused to comply. Some were imprisoned. Two hundred women stormed a castle to secure the release of two pastors. The women were trounced.[20] Other pastors were exiled. They took refuge with John's brother Karl of Södermanland. He was as much concerned as John for church unity, but whereas John wished to unite the Lutherans and the Catholics, Karl hoped rather to effect a union with the Calvinists that the two Protestant varieties might present a solid phalanx against Rome. His refusal to yield to the authority of his brother menaced the stability of the crown.

All the more reason, then, why John should seek to recover his wife's share of the Neapolitan legacy of her mother! In the interim the status of the legacy had changed. Cardinal Hosius had suggested to the three sisters that the case could be better handled at Rome if conducted by only one sister. They concurred and

Sofia and Katarina made over their shares to Anna with the private understanding that she would restore to each a third. Then another shift in the political situation reversed the arrangement. The possibility emerged that Anna could not inherit anything because she married the newly elected king of Poland, Stephen Batory, who was claimed to be a heretic because as ruler of Transylvania he was a feudatory of the Sultan. Then, Sofia having died, Anna made everything over to Katarina with the assurance of reimbursement. But at that point Batory was reconciled with Rome. In that case Anna, his wife, could inherit and Katarina proposed to go back to the agreement of equal division. But John would have none of it.

Then ensued a piece of incredible chicanery on his part. While Katarina instructed her representative to do nothing at Rome prejudicial to her sister, John told his emissary to press for the ultimate penny. Anna would not believe that her sister could treat her so and Katarina grieved to be under suspicion and, to clear herself, made over everything to Anna. John had to retreat and cleared himself with Anna by laying the blame on his Italian representative.[21]

Next came a more distressing rift not simply between the sisters but between the kingdoms.[22] After a war of Sweden and Poland together against Russia, Poland had made a separate peace and had taken for herself Livonia and the port Narva, which in the struggle had been won by the Swedes. The Polish ambassador came to reconcile John to the agreement by pointing out that for the duration of the treaty these territories in Polish hands would be free from Russian attack and if Russia struck at Sweden at some other point Poland would rally to her side. John, in a rage, swore that neither the wisdom of Solomon or the eloquence of Cicero would ever affright him and induce him to cede Livonia.

"Well, then," said the Polish envoy, "may I talk to the queen?"

"Go ahead," and John stalked out.

The envoy pointed out to her how important it was that cordial relations be maintained between her domain and that of her sister, particularly because her son Sigismund might some day be the king of Poland. Katarina replied that she had often longed for an alliance but every plan had gone the way of smoke. She was then reminded that Poland was in a position to have recourse to constraint and she would find war very grievous. If her husband needed more time for consideration, Poland could wait. But if John were thinking of war, then let him think long.

Katarina answered, "God alone knows how I suffer and how I am absolutely devastated by the lack of amity between the two kingdoms. I don't think I can influence my husband, but grief over it all will send me to the grave."

Most distressing to her was the recoil of her husband. The Jesuits, who had already accomplished so much clandestinely, came out into the open on the advice of the legate who hoped thereby to force John's hand and drive him to full submission. The reverse was true. He renounced his conversion to Rome and expelled the Jesuits. Perhaps even more distressing to the queen was that, whereas the son Sigismund sided with her, the daughter Anna lined up with her father.[23] One of the factors in the Thirty Years war was the conflict between the Catholic and the Lutheran descendants of Katarina.

Another factor in John's reversal was that all hope of the Neapolitan legacy had evaporated. There never had been a live chance. Once before an observer had said, "Though the queen should become a nun and the king a Jesuit, they would never get a cent." [24] Still another point was that the relatively tractable Pope Gregory XIII was succeeded by the utterly intractable Sixtus V.

When Katarina died in 1583 the Catholics desired to celebrate a Mass for her soul. John consented but did not attend. Sigismund attended. Presumably Anna did not. The widowed John, after two years, married a staunchly Lutheran girl of sixteen. The hope of the restoration of Catholicism in Sweden was definitely gone.

With the death of Batory the throne of Poland was again vacant. Anna, his widow, threw all of her influence in favor of her nephew and he was elected as Sigismund III. Mindful of his youthful oath never to receive the sacrament at the hands of a heretic on pain of eternal damnation, he set himself to advance the Counter-Reformation. When his sister Anna came to visit him and began making converts to Lutheranism, he shipped her back to Sweden. In 1592 John died and then by dynastic succession rather than election, Sigismund became the king also of Sweden. The dream of Kromer was fulfilled, the union of the two kingdoms under a king at once a scion of the Vasas and the Jagellons. But the other half of the dream that Sweden should be made Catholic wrecked the first half. Sigismund tried by force to Catholicize Sweden. His uncle Charles rose up against him to become Charles IX and he was the father of Gustavus Adolphus.[25]

## CHRONOLOGY

| | |
|---|---|
| 1526 | Birth of Katarina |
| 1560 | Erik becomes king |
| 1562 | John married to Katarina |
| 1566 | Birth of Sigismund |
| 1568 | John and Charles depose Erik |
| 1569 | Coronation of John |
| 1572 | Death of Pius V succeeded by Gregory XIII |
| 1575 | Death of Sofia of Brunswick |
| 1577 | Death of Erik XIV<br>The new liturgy |
| 1580 | Two hundred women storm a castle to release pastors |
| 1581 | The Augsburg Confession in Swedish |
| 1582 | Dispute with Poland over Narva |
| 1583 | Death of Katarina |
| 1585 | John marries Gunilla Bielke<br>Death of Gregory XIII succeeded by Sixtus V |
| 1587 | Sigismund III, king of Poland |
| 1592 | Death of John |
| 1596 | Death of Anna in Poland |
| 1600 | Deposition of Sigismund in Sweden |

Portions of the Funeral Procession of John III
Clergy to the left

## BIBLIOGRAPHY

An excellent study of Swedish history in this period is that of Michael
Roberts, *The Early Vasas . . . 1523-1611* (Cambridge, Eng., 1968).

Swedish Church history for the reign of Gustavus Vasa is covered by
Conrad Bergendoff, *Olavus Petri . . . 1521-52* (New York, 1928).

For the entire period see Hjalmar Holmquist, *Svenska Kyrkans Historia* III (Stockholm, 1933). In two parts with separate pagination.

A more detailed account of the period of John III is that of Augustin
Theiner, *La Suède et le Saint-Siège. . . .* 3 volumes, tr. Jean Cohen (Paris 1842), rabidly Catholic, scrupulously accurate with a considerable
appendix of documents in volume III.

Extensive treatments are given in the works of three Finnish scholars:
Henry Biaudet and his pupils, K. I. and Liisi Karttunen, all writing in
French. Biaudet's doctoral dissertation is entitled *Le Saint Siège et la
Suède . . .* (Paris, 1906). Two volumes of supporting documents came
out in different series. The first with the title of the dissertation appeared in *Documents concernants l'histoire des pays du Nord (Suomen
historiallelnen seura) (Helsingfors, Paris)*, 1, 1906. Summarizes documents. Copy New York Public Library. The second volume with complete texts appeared in *Ètudes Romaines* III (Geneva, 1912). Copies
New York Public Library and University of Utah. K. I. Karttunen's dis-

sertation was *Jean III et Stefan Batory* (Helsinki, 1911). Liisi Karttunen published, *Antonio Possevino* (Lausanne, 1908).

The above three scholars published a series of articles in *Annales Academiae Scientiarum Fennicae,* Ser. B, Volumes 1-2, 1909-11: Biaudet, "Les Nonciatures permanentes"; "Sixte-Quint et la Candidature de Sigismund de Suède. . . ." K. I. Karttunen, on "Alamanni," Liisi Karttunen, "Grégoire XIII comme polititien. . . ." Volumes 5-6, 1912: Biaudet on "Brancaccio," and K. I. Karttunen's thesis. Volumes 7-8, 1913: Biaudet, "Correspondence de . . . Zuniga," "Jean III de Suède et sa cour," "Gustaf Erikson Vasa."

A number of documents are included in Joann Baazius, *Inventarum Ecclesiae Sveo-Gothorum* . . . (Link, 1642). Beinecke Library at Yale. Documents are summarized in *Johannis Messenii Scondia Illustrata* (Stockholm, 1700). Yale Library.

The correspondence of Cardinal Hosius is in Stanislaus Hosjusz, *Opera Omnia* (Koln, 1584), Beinecke Library, Yale.

Kromer's account of the captivity of John and Katarina is described by Claude Backvis, "Histoire Veredique de la piteuse aventure du duc Jean de Finlande et la Princesse Catherine," *Revue des Études Slaves* XXIX (1952), 16-23. The original Polish has been edited by Alexander Kraushar in *Bibljoteka Pisarzow Polskich* XX (1892) issued by the Polska Akademia Kraków with the title "Historya prawdzwia o przgodzie załosnej książęcia Finlandzkiego Jana i krolewny Katarzyny."

The work of Oskar Garstein, *Rome and the Counter-Reformation in Scandinavia* (Bergen, Norway, and Oxford Univ. Press), vol. 1, 1963), is a very detailed and thoroughly documented account of the efforts of Rome to reclaim Sweden. Vivid pictures are given of the labors of the Jesuit Swede Norvegus and the Legate Possevino. But since this little sketch centers on Katarina and the text must not be cluttered with names I have introduced only Hosius on the Roman side.

The contribution of Katarina and John to Renaissance architecture in Sweden is covered by August Hahr, "Drottning Katarina Jagellonica" *Kungl. Humanistiska Vetenskapssamfundet i Uppsala, Skrifter* XXXIV, 1 (1940).

The Italian legacy of Queen Bona is described in detail by Klemens Kantecki, *Die Neopolitanischen Summen* (Posen, 1882), copy at Harvard.

On the influence of Cassander see Paula Broder, *Georg Cassanders Vermittlungsversuche zwichen Protestanten und Katholiken* (Marburg, 1931) and Maria Elisabeth Notte, *Georgius Cassander en zijn Oecumenisch Streven* (Nijmwegen, 1951).

## NOTES

1. Biaudet, "Jean III et sa cour," p. 23; Theiner II, 284, III, 387.
2. Macrin Kromer, see bibliography.
3. Roberts, pp. 246, 148, Biaudet, "Gustaf Erikson Vasa."

4. Hahr, see bibliography.
5. Roberts, p. 274.
6. Bergendoff, especially pp. 223, 235, 244, 249.
7. Roberts, p. 275.
8. Baazius III, vi, 331.
9. First observed by Messenius, pp. 27, 47.
10. Theiner II, 284.
11. *Ibid.,* p. 295.
12. See Kentecki in Bona bibliography, Biaudet "Brancaccio," and Kartunen, "Grégorei XIII comme politien."
13. Hosius, *Opera Omnia,* Ep. 1777, also in Baazius III, 12.
14. Theiner III, 78-79, and Garstein on Sigismund p. 193, on John p. 136.
15. Theiner II, 114.
16. *Ibid.,* III, 91-101.
17. *Ibid.,* III, 387.
18. *Ibid.,* II, 76.
19. *Ibid.,* II, 76-78.
20. *Ibid.,* III, 181-2.
21. See note 12.
22. K. I. Karttunen, "Alamanni."
23. Garstein, pp. 201, 209, 212, 239.
24. Theiner II, 142.
25. See Roberts.

# HUNGARY AND TRANSYLVANIA

Maria of Hungary and Bohemia was a Hapsburg, the sister of the Emperor Charles V, of Ferdinand of Austria, Elizabeth (Isabel) of Denmark and Eleanore of Portugal. Born in 1505, Maria, while still in the cradle, was promised to the as yet unborn son (provided he turned out to be a *he*) of Wladislaw of Bohemia and Hungary. The babe proved to be Louis. The couple were publically betrothed when she was ten, crowned and married when she was seventeen. The young husband, after only four years of marriage, was lost in the battle with the Turks at Mohacs in 1526. With him the flower of the Hungarian nobility was wiped out. Maria remained for life a widow.[1]

On the death of her husband she received a letter of consolation from Martin Luther, who dedicated to her four of his sermons on the Psalms, saying that he had been moved so to do by the news of her inclination to the gospel. His thought initially was to give her reason "to rejoice and be exceeding glad. But now that your land is ravaged and your husband fallen, I must write in another vein." [2]

The rumor that she was inclined to the gospel was entirely correct.[3] A representative of Rome reported the rumor that the king and queen were Lutherans. The writer discounted the rumor though ready to admit that among the Germans at her court there might be some Lutherans. The queen favored them not as Lutherans but as Germans. He had talked with their

Maria of Hungary

majesties and found them sound in the faith and ready to investigate reports of deviance. Yet when the pope made an alliance with France against her brother the Emperor Charles, Maria said that if the pope so behaved she and all her court would be Lutherans. She had Lutheran ministers in her circle and intervened to save Lutherans from imprisonment and death. At the same time her brother Ferdinand and her husband Louis were issuing severe edicts against the Lutherans. She felt that she was being persecuted for her faith and composed a poem which has the ring of Luther's *Mighty Fortress*. It is an acrostic. The first letters of the three stanzas combined form her name Maria. I have brashly attempted to reproduce the rhyme scheme, the meter and the sense.

> MAy I reverse not cast aside.
> The world cannot me abide
> Because of my believing.
> Full well I know
> God is my sword,
> And of my Lord
> None is me relieving.

Maria and Louis II of Hungary

But for a mite
He holds his spite
Till with a blow
He lays them low,
Who his word are stealing.

RIght well at hand my case I see.
Know right well how weak I be.
God lets me be affrighted.
No force endures,
For God insures
That it shall be benighted.
The good can't fail.
It makes me hale.
Thereto I stand
With life and land,
For I shall be requited.

As one and one must equal twice
So sure is Jesus Christ.
As it were yours, you take my woe,
Nor will let go.
Hold back the foe what'er betide.
I cannot but essay this road,
Support the load.
World take the field.
God is my shield.
The field is ours. Be you defied.

The authenticity of this poem has been impugned on the ground that it is in German whereas she normally wrote in French.[4] True, but sometimes also in German. We have the testimony of the margrave of Brandenburg that in 1529 she composed the poem to voice her dismay over the persecution inflicted by her brother.[5]

Erasmus likewise solaced the widow.[6] "War," he began "is the greatest of all evils. For earthquakes, floods, lightning and plagues no one is responsible but what so atrocious as that man should immolate man! War carries off the youngest and the

Hungary in Flames

best. War makes widows, severing the most intimate of bonds.
You are bereft of your Louis, young, generous, of noble lineage,
endowed with all the qualities of a prince. You had only a few
years together. You were not at hand to give the parting kiss. He
has left you no child in whom to see his likeness. I will not offer
you the consolations of the Stoics who believe not in the life to
come. I will rather set before you an absorbing career.

"Christ is the King of Kings to whom we must all give account.
Women can lead as examples. I will not discuss the relative
merits of virginity, widowhood and marriage. Each has its role.
Let your court be marked by piety, simplicity and sobriety. Do
your utmost to avoid war. Shun discourse with no one. Be ready
to talk with heretics, Jews and Turks. Like St. Elizabeth, combine
the dignity of a duchess with the piety of a nun.

"I have already dedicated some of my works to members of
your family: to your brother Charles the Emperor the tract on
*The Education of the Christian Prince;* to your brother Ferdinand the *Paraphrase of the Gospel of John;* to your aunt Catherine of Aragon the *Treatise on Matrimony.* I received the sug-

gestion of inscribing to you this delineation of the role of the Christian widow from that most excellent man, John Henkel, whose admirable zeal in proclaiming gospel truth is due to your benevolence. May the Lord bestow upon your highness every spiritual joy."

The reference to Henckel [7] introduces us to the one who is credited with having turned Maria from the intransigeance of Luther to the moderation of Erasmus. After 1525 her efforts were directed not to the propagation of Lutheranism but to the reconciliation of the parties. Henkel was a disciple of Erasmus and esteemed a letter from him to be of greater value than a bishopric. A man of great learning, he had no ambition for preferment, and when Maria offered to make him a bishop, would have none of it. She pulled him away from his parish and tried to keep him constantly at court. Like Erasmus, he was averse to constraint in religion and deplored the persecution which Ferdinand visited upon all varieties of Protestants. Some were imprisoned, some beaten with rods in public squares, some banished, some burned. Henkel never identified himself with Luther, but like Erasmus, would never call him a heretic and would never discourage any from reading his books.

The liberalism which Maria may well have imbibed from Henkel brought her into tension with her brothers. We have a fairly extensive correspondence with Ferdinand. Her tone is affectionate, at the same time firm in dissent from his policy in religion.[8] He remonstrated with her that Luther had dedicated to her his sermons on the Psalms.

"I had nothing to do with that," she replied. "I can't stop him from dedicating to whom he pleases. I will not prejudice the reputation of our house."

Ferdinand answered, "I know you can't prevent Luther from dedicating books. I hope he won't dedicate one to me, stuffed with praises that I accept the doctrine he calls the gospel. I hope you won't read his damned books, nor let any of your circle have them. Scotch the rumor that you have Lutheran leanings. My dear sister, I hope you will forgive me. I must discharge my conscience."

Maria replied, "With God's help I intend to remain a good Christian. It is a long time since I have read Luther, and, in accord with your admonition, I will take care not to read him. If any one says that I am a Lutheran and not in accord with the ruling of the Church, I confess I did eat meat during Lent. That was to ward off an illness from which I am not yet fully recovered. The Father of Discord has been trying to alienate you and me. Do not believe malicious tongues. With God's help I will be your loyal sister till death."

He answered, "I do not question that you are loyal and I will not let any one sow dissension."

But Ferdinand was no less minded to wipe out heresy. He expressed to his brother Charles the hope that peace with France would make possible a joint campaign to extirpate "the heresies arising from the Lutheran sect."[9] By this phrase he meant the Zwinglians and the Anabaptists. Maria in May of 1528 [10] reported to him that in her territory a preacher had come denouncing the holy sacrament and baptism (of infants). "I ordered him to leave and he did, but many had been seduced by his teaching. Therefore I sent a preacher, well versed in Scripture, to refute this teaching. I was told that this preacher was a Lutheran. But since he was opposed to this sect, I let him preach. He gave two sermons, one on the Eucharist and one on baptism. He refuted those who repeat baptism and refuse to take an oath. As for the chalice in the Eucharist, he quoted the words 'Drink ye all of it' and said we must do what Christ enjoins. I do not want people with these opinions (that is the sectaries) at my court. I will confess to you, as to my confessor, that I read a tract of Luther against these people, though you told me not to read him at all. But since his tract is against them, I thought you would approve. I am sending it to you. What he says about baptism and the sacrament of the altar is excellent. If I have displeased you I humbly beseech you to pardon me."

Ferdinand answered,[11] "You tell me you dismissed that preacher who rejected the sacrament of the altar and baptism. You should have punished him according to his deserts. You would then have deflated the suspicion that you are a Lutheran. As for your sending a Lutheran preacher to refute their errors,

I will say that to close one wound you open three or four. If this gets to the ear of the emperor and other Christian princes, especially those who love our house, that you have a Lutheran court preacher, condemned not only by the emperor but by the pope and the Christian Church as a heretic, contravening the commands and edicts of the emperor, and you his sister who should obey and comply . . . imagine what a bad example you give! As for the articles he preaches, I am not competent to discuss them. That's not my specialty. But it were better that he should not preach and you should not listen. As for that book, his errors are condemned as heretical and there are plenty of good books and good preachers without bringing in Lutherans. As a confessor I spare not the penitent. And besides, I do my duty as a good brother, concerned for your honor and the honor of our house."

The next year Ferdinand wrote to her that she had given him to understand there were Anabaptists in Moravia.[12]

"I hope you will inform me more exactly," he wrote, "for you realize the evil that will ensue if these heresies invade. You have encouraged preaching against these damnable heresies. Very good. In the future suppress them utterly, for in my opinion these are the worst errors that ever were."

She answered,[13] "You tell me to drive out one of their leaders. I have sent my chaplain to convert him. The man is so obdurate as to ask for nothing better than death. To tell you the truth, I would not advise you to touch his life, for these people go to martyrdom with great joy. You ask me to give you details about their assemblies. I think that as a woman I'd better not meddle in this. Others can inform you. In accord with your command I will not let the man preach. My own preacher is on leave. I hope that he will soon come back and that his ministry will bear fruit."

The next year (1530) the Diet met at Augsburg in part to resolve the religious difficulty. The Emperor Charles was in attendance. So also was his sister Maria. Luther could not come because of the ban; Erasmus for some other reason. Melanchthon led the moderate Protestants. Among the Erasmian Catholics was John Henckel, who had never been expelled. He squelched the blustering truculence of the immoderate John Eck.[14] Maria, who had been commanded never even to read Luther, compiled a set of questions to be sent to him via Henkel and Melanchthon. In an accompanying note Melanchthon said that "the sister of the emperor, a woman of heroic mold, distinguished for piety and modesty, is trying to mollify her brother on our behalf but is constrained to make a modest and discreet approach." [15]

One of the questions put to Luther was whether the Eucharist must invariably be received with the wine as well as the bread, or, in lands where only the bread was allowed, might one conform in public and take the wine in a private celebration. Luther would have nothing half way. Either both or nothing save communion in the heart.

The Augsburg Confession, composed by the moderating Melanchthon, was still too Protestant for the Catholics. The emperor gave the Lutherans a year in which to submit. If they then refused, he would resort to war and would have done so had he not been involved in other wars for a quarter of a century.

In the year after the diet (1531) the regent of the Netherlands died. She was Marguerite of Austria, the aunt of Charles, Ferdinand, Maria, Elizabeth and Eleanor. A new appointment was needed. Charles turned to Maria and wrote: [16]

> My dear sister: I am sure I do not need to inform you of the death of our aunt who was to me as a mother. This is a double blow because of the vacancy in the regency of the Netherlands. I know of no one more competent to replace her than yourself. If I had known that her death was imminent I would have broached the matter to you while we were both at Augsburg. I hope you can be ready to leave as speedily as possible. On the matter of marriage you will not be pressed. Now as to the rectitude of your faith. I have no misgiving. Otherwise I would not have asked you. But some of your household may be suspect. I must tell you that, whereas some laxity may be allowed in Germany, it is not so in the Netherlands. [Charles was quite right on that point. In the Netherlands he had first been able to enforce the edict

of Worms against the Lutherans because in this region he was the local ruler by hereditary right and was not encumbered by such another as Frederick the Wise. The first Lutheran martyrdoms took place in the Netherlands.] It were better not to bring with you any of your household, and for the additional reason that the Netherlanders do not like foreigners. Rebuild your staff from natives.

Maria was not at all happy over this proposal. She had made that quite clear earlier when Ferdinand had sounded her feeling.[17] Her health was precarious and she had no enthusiasm for the draconian program of her brother. Her feeling was like that of Erasmus, who left the Netherlands rather than be turned into a butcher. But Erasmus was only a councillor of the emperor. She was his sister and obligated to assume the offices of the state. She consented out of loyalty to her brother.

For nearly twenty-five years she was the regent in the Netherlands. Repeated edicts against the Lutherans were issued with increasing severity. She signed them, for she regarded the "heretics" as rebels, though deserving of compassion. She would mitigate sentences and connive at escapes.[18] The liberal Cardinal Marone said in 1539 that she was a "most obstinate woman who, out of her own head, showed leniency toward Lutherans."[19] She was spared compliance with the rigors of the Spanish Inquisition, introduced by her nephew Philip II, for on the abdication of Charles in 1555, she accompanied him to Spain and there died in 1558. Her suffering for the faith was not that of the thumbscrew and the stake, but the anguish of the tortured heart, seeking to emulate the mercy of God and sustain the rule of his servants of the house of Hapsburg.

## NOTES

1. Biographical sketches in the *Allgemeine Deutsche Biographie*. Georg Loesche, "Die evangelischen Fürstinnen im Hause Habsburg," *Jahrbuch der Gesellschaft für Geschichte des Protestantismus in Oesterreich* XV (1904), 5-21.
George Heiss, "Politik und Ratgeber Maria von Ungarn in den Jahren 1521-31," *Mittheilungen des Instituts für Oestreich. Geschichtsforschung*, LXXXII (1874), 119-180.

2. *Weimare Ausgabe* XIX, p. 542 ff.

3. Wilhelm Stracke, *Die Anfänge der Königin Maria von Ungarn späteren Stadthalterin Karls V. in den Niederlanden* (Göttingen, 1940). Citing *Monumenta Vaticana Hungariae* II,1 (Budapest, 1884), pp. 23, 28, 133, 139, 159, 160.

4. "Die Korrespondenz Ferdinands I," ed. Wilhelm Bauer und Robert Lacroix, 2 vols. (Vienna, 1897-8), *Veröffentlichungen der Kommission für neuere Geschichte Oesterreichs.* Letter no. 13.

5. The text, discussion and the letter of the margrave in Theodor Kolde, "Margraf Georg von Brandenburg und das Glaubenslied der Königen Maria von Ungarn," *Beiträge zur bayerischen Kirchengeschichte,* II (1896), 62-89.

6. *Opera Omnia* (Lug. 1704), V, 723-766.

7. Georg Bauch, "Dr. Johann Henckel der Hofprediger der Königen Maria von Ungarn," *Ungarische Revue* (1884), 599-627.

8. *Op. cit.* note 4 supra. nos. 44, 45, 49, 54, 55.

9. *Ibid.,* No. 131.

10. *Ibid.,* No. 183.

11. *Ibid.,* No. 207.

12. *Ibid.,* No. 298.

13. *Ibid.,* No. 302.

14. *Erasmi Epistolae* IX, No. 2392, p. 58.

15. Melanchthon, *Corp. Ref.* II, No. 770, p. 178. No. 808, p. 233.

16. *Correspondenz des Kaisers Karl V,* ed. Karl Lanz, (Leipzig, 1894). Bd. 1, No. 156.

17. Note 5 above, No. 154, p. 190.

18. See Loesche, note 1 above.

19. Erich Roth, *Die Reformation in Siebenbürgen* (1962), p. 12, note 12. Die Königen, eine donna obstitanissima et di suo cervello begünstige die Lutherana.

Queen Isabella and her signature

# Isabella Zapolya

Isabella Zapolya was the firstborn of Bona Sforza and Sigismund Stary and the sister of Katarina of Sweden, Sophia of Brunswick, Anna of Poland and Sigismund Augustus. Of her early life I have been able to find only what can be inferred from her accomplishments and behavior. She certainly learned Polish from her father, Italian from her mother and Latin from her tutors. She loved the chase, the dance and gorgeous festivities with opulent display. One early historian called her dissolute, another sagacious and one who knew her said she was difficult unless one humored her whims.[1]

At the age of twenty she was married to John Zapolya, connected by family but not by blood. His sister had been her father's first wife; that is Barbara Zapolya had been the first queen of Sigismund Stary. John Zapolya, at the time of the marriage with Isabella, was fifty-two and disinclined to wed until a fellow Pannonian insisted that the perpetuation of the precious gem of his blood would cast glory on their land.[2] A few years earlier Bona and Sigismund would scarcely have considered the alliance prestigious because John was virtually in exile. He had been the *voivode* or lieutenant of Transylvania under Louis II of Hungary. When the king fell in flight from the battle of Mohacs in 1526, two claimants contested the succession. The one was Ferdinand in the name of his widowed sister, Maria. The other was Zapolya with the support of the Transylvanians, or Siebenbürgers, as they were called. War followed. Zapolya, defeated, fled to Poland. This was in 1529.

Here he fell in with an astute diplomat, the monk Martinuzzi, who maneuvered to replace him on the throne. A decade of strife issued in the treaty of Varda (1539) whereby the land was divided. The western section went to Ferdinand as King of Hungary, the eastern to Zapolya as King of Transylvania, and the middle to the Sultan. A clause stipulated that should Zapolya die without issue his portion should revert to Ferdinand. If he did have issue, the son should be only the *voivode* of Transylvania. Now that Zapolya was king, the marriage would appear advantageous to Bona and Sigismund Stary, the more so because Transylvania was a buffer between Christendom and Islam, and besides there was the possibility that the Hapsburgs might be ousted. We recall the rage of Bona when Sigismund Augustus married Barbara Radziwill and thwarted the scheme to unite him with Anna of Ferrara, the granddaughter of a king of France, which might then be inclined to induce the Sultan to place her daughter on the throne of Hungary.

The treaty of Varda was upset when Isabella, at the end of a year of marriage, gave birth in 1540 to a son, named Sigismund for his grandfather and uncle. On the arrival of an heir, Zapolya, with only a month to live, repudiated the treaty and demanded that his son inherit his title. When the father died, Isabella took up the campaign for the infant.

She received from her parents condolence with hints of intervention. The father wrote,[3]

> Serenissima Princeps, filia nostra charissima: Right hearty thanks for informing us of the birth of your son. But this news is tinged with sadness as we learn of the death of your Majesty's Serene husband. Do not allow yourself to be crushed by grief. The course of prudence is that reason should rule the emotions. It becomes a prince to bear with composure that which cannot be altered. To succumb to immoderate weeping is to contest the will of God, whose judgments are a great abyss. Our hope and confidence lie in his unfailing mercy. He will assuredly not desert you and

Vier warhafftige Missi=
uen/eine der frawen Isabella Königin vnd
nachgelassene wittib in Vngern/wie vn=
trewlich der Türck vnd die iren
mit ir vmbgangen.

Die ander/eines so in der belegerung bey
der Königin im Schloß gewest/wie es mit Ofen/
vor vñ nach der belegerung ergangen.

Die dritte/eines Vngern von Gran/
wie es yetz zu Ofen zugehe.

Die vierdte/des Türckischen Tyran=
nen an die Sibenbürger.

Auß dem Latein ins
Teutsch gebracht.

A Tract by Isabella Zapolya against the perfidy of the Turks

your sorrow shall be crowned with joy. The lot of man is that sorrow be mingled with joy as joy with sorrow. The Fount of all goodness, in taking your husband, has given you the loveliest son that in fondling and kissing you may alleviate your grief. In place of a father the infant has a grandfather. Consult us in all arrangements. From Wilna, 15 August, 1540.

Bona wrote a month later: [4]

Forgive us that we have been so long in writing. We could not find a suitable courier. Suffer not yourself to be mired in grief. After the sorrow of the night comes the joy of the morning. Your parents are ever ready to stand by. 1 October, 1540.

Ferdinand protested against the disavowal of the treaty of Varda and laid siege (1541) to the city of Olah where Isabella was in residence in the castle. Three contemporary tracts (published in 1542) related the event: [5]

The first is a preface exhorting Christians, since the arm of man has failed, to invoke divine aid to overcome the Turkish tyrant, whose perfidy is so manifest that Christians should never again invite the Turk to repel the Germans. Let all Christians rather unite against the foe.

Next comes a page from the pen of Isabella deploring Turkish deception, but rejoicing to learn that the Siebenbürgers have elected her son as the King of Transylvania.

Third, we have an eyewitness account of the siege and negotiations. Here is a condensation.

"We are sorry not to have communicated sooner but the bearer of a letter was in danger of losing a head. The anxiety and extremity of this siege defy imagination. One did not dare to venture out for a drink, let alone for provender. The wall was several times breached, but the foe repulsed. Tunneling under the walls was intercepted. Our men were so emboldened as to make a sortie and smite the foe beyond the walls. The Germans built a bridge across the Danube but the wind cast it down. At that moment Mohamet Bez Bassa arrived and the Turks lifted the

Newe zeyttung / von Kayserli=
cher vnd küncklicher Mayestat /
So yezunt geschehē/ vnd gemacht ist worden / zů
Prag/ auch von dem Frantzhosen/ vnd Turcken/
vñ sambt dem Graff Weyda/ gehandelt
vnd vrkůntlich außgangen. jm
M.D.XXXviij. jar dē
24. Aprilis.
✱✱
✱

A Battle with the Turks

siege. They lauded our steadfastness. The queen and her councillors were given some of the cattle plundered along the way. Sufficient food was supplied. We went into the Turkish camp and were received with friendliness.

"Shortly the Turks brought their armada up the river. Three thousand Czechs and two thousand Germans were slaughtered. (Are these figures reliable?) Six hundred were held as captives, some of whom Isabella ransomed. Part of the German force, abandoning their armaments, marched off in formation with flags flying.

"Presents were sent after a week to the young king, four gold necklaces, three Turkish horses, splendidly caparisoned, their saddles studded with gold. The queen's councillors received robes. The Sultan sent word to her that he wished to see her son. She was frightened and suggested to her advisers that she go alone with presents or, if this would not do, that she take the boy. They told her to comply. The lad was taken by a nurse and two old women in a chariot of gold preceded by councillors. The Sultan sent courtiers to meet and greet them. They were conducted to a tent alongside of his, and two marshals entered with silver scepters. The child began to cry and the nurse held him. Then the councillors were taken to another tent to confer with the Sultan, and what it was all about I do not know.

"The Sultan announced that he would keep Ofen. Our leaders were appalled but dared not speak. The mayor of Ofen was called in and heard the news in silence. The Janissaries then marched into the city. This move had evidently been planned, for they could not have made an impromptu entry. Next came dinner. The prince was placed between the nurse and the two women. I sat opposite. We were made to eat sitting on the ground which we took to be a great insult. A marshal then informed us the child might be returned. It was night and we were conducted by torches. We did not think it proper to present the Turks to the queen by night and dismissed them. A number of the councillors were retained to discuss whether the queen and prince should be taken to Constantinople or be left with the councillors. The latter was decided, thank God. The queen thanked the Sultan for returning her son, begged to be taken under his protection, promised not to remarry and sent a present to his daughter. He promised to do his best for her.

"The Janissaries commanded the keeper of the castle to turn over the keys. He went in tears to the queen who told him to do what he was told. The prisons were opened and the inmates sent to the Sultan. This proved that Turks were not being held captive. Plundering began in the city. The queen was told not to fear. She should have Siebenbürgen and the land beyond up to the Teyss. Then, on the pretext that this area was rebellious, the promise was cancelled. Presents were sent to the queen and prince, and horses promised for their return, but she had to buy oxen out of her own funds. The Turks went into the church of Our Lady and gave thanks to their god for the victory. The queen wept. An escort of Janissaries with 150 horses guarded our journey. We slept in tents. The queen had to take orders from the Sultan. The weather was wet. A number died of the pestilence. All this we had to endure in addition to the siege. God visited this upon us for our sins. May his name be praised, for we hope that by his grace he will comfort us with his mercy."

Isabella ruled as queen regent only in Transylvania for the decade of 1541-1551. She was aided, or rather manipulated, in the administration both at home and abroad by her prime minister so to speak, that monk who had once helped her husband, Martinuzzi.[6] He was a statesman of real calibre, who envisioned the reintegration of all Hungary. This would require, to begin with, the unification of Transylvania itself. Here, too, there were three sections: the Saxons who spoke German; the Szeklers, a Magyar stock who entered the land prior to the Hungarians and the magnates, or nobles, mostly Hungarian.

The divisions were intensified by religion, seeing that the Saxons became at first Lutheran, the Hungarians Calvinist and the Szeklers remained Catholic. If all these could act as a unit the more difficult problem could be faced of harmonizing Isabella, Ferdinand and Suleiman. This was a slippery undertaking because no one trusted anyone. A contemporary remarked that princes did not believe the oaths of neighbors and allies. If a concession were made to one, the others suspected treachery.

# SENTENTIAE

## EX OMNIBVS OPERIBVS
## DIVI AVGVSTINI
## DECERPTAE.

## ANNO.    M. D. XXXIX.

The Coat of Arms of John and Isabella Zapolya on the Title Page of a work of Augustine edited by the humanist scholar and Lutheran minister, Johannes Honterus.

Martinuzzi, acting for Isabella, yielded so much to Ferdinand that he had him made a cardinal. Isabella was not pleased. To the Turk Martinuzzi yielded Buda. Ferdinand was not pleased. He did, indeed, grasp the grand plan and saw the need for concessions, but at the same time instructed his general to have an eye open for any double dealing, and, if need be, to have recourse to the ultimate remedy. The general, who did not grasp the grand plan, disposed of Martinuzzi by assassination. That marked the end of the effort to reunite Hungary. Ferdinand then resolved to unite all not in the hands of the Turk. He fell upon Isabella and drove her and her son again to Poland.

The next four years (1551-1555) were spent bickering.[7] Ferdinand had granted her by way of indemnity the assurance of maintenance. She complained that the castle where she lodged was dilapidated. The meadows had no cattle large or small. The fish pond had been broken and drained. With her own funds and the bounty of her mother she had purchased seed grain, beds, tables, chairs and kitchen utensils. From all taxes, tributes and military obligations she should be free. An understanding was reached in 1553 and Ferdinand's daughter was betrothed to young Sigismund. But Isabella still had her eye on Siebenbürgen and both she and Ferdinand were in touch with the Porte. Their embassies encountered each other in Constantinople and her envoy indiscreetly let Ferdinand's ambassador know that Isabella was beseeching Suleiman on her metaphorical knees to deliver her from Ferdinand. There was even a rumor that he was plotting to assassinate her son. We do not know whether she believed it, but she would scarcely have found it incredible in view of the fate of Martinuzzi. In any case Ferdinand let her know he would send her no more money unless she renounced all claim to Siebenbürgen, and she answered she would not renounce all claim to Siebenbürgen unless he sent the money. At that juncture word came that France would give her support and Suleiman promised that if she and her son would return he would restore everything captured since the death of her husband. The Siebenbürgers were prompted to issue an invitation. Isabella and her son reentered on 22 October, 1556. Transylvania was now a separate country. Isabella continued as queen dowager until her death in 1559 and her son as king until his death in 1571.

The prevailingly political history thus far given prompts a question why Isabella should have been included among women in active religious roles. But she did have convictions and feelings. She wept over the desecration of the church of Our Lady. As a queen she could not avoid religious issues. We have mentioned that the three sections of the land were characterized by three varieties of religion. The Saxons were Lutheran. The Hungarians turned to Calvin quite possibly because he was not German, and the Szeklers in their villages were addicted to the traditional Catholicism. The answer to such diversity was religious liberty. Isabella, whatever her convictions, may have been the readier to refrain from persecution because of the Polish parallel. But the decisive factor was the Turk, who looked upon all Christians as unbelievers and tolerated all indiscriminately, lest a tributary state be unable to pay tribute because rent by wars of religion. In any case, Isabella is the first ruler to issue an edict of universal toleration. The state would not impose a creed. The sects must not molest each other. This meant that the Protestants could not expropriate the goods of the Catholics. The edict reads:

> In as much as we and our most Serene Son have graciously consented to the urgent petition of the Lords of the realm that each observe the faith of his preference with new or ancient ceremonies, permitting freedom of choice to each according to preference, provided no harm be done to any, that neither the followers of the new religion are to do despite to the old, nor are the old in any way to injure the followers of the new, therefore the Lords of the realm, in order to promote concord among the churches and to dispel the controversies occasioned by the rise of the evangelical doctrine, have decreed the calling of a national council where devout ministers of God and other eminent members of the nobility may engage in discussion of sincere doctrine that under God dissensions and diversities of religion may be overcome.[8]

Such a proclamation not only recognized what had already

happened but opened the way for more. Unitarianism was to become the prevailing religion of the land. Isabella certainly did not foster this, but unwittingly contributed by favor shown to the men who started the trend. They were two Italian doctors. Blandrata was a specialist in female diseases who had been the physician to Bona Sforza, then to Isabella and finally to her son. Blandrata's views on the Trinity were tentative and mild. He would not go beyond the source of Christian doctrine, the New Testament itself. And here he did not find the terminology of the Nicene creed which reluctantly employed non-scriptural terminology in order to exclude the opinions of the Arians who would accept Scripture interpreted in their own way. Blandrata was influenced also by the scholastic disputations which had revolted Michael Servetus burned at Geneva for his denial of the orthodox Trinitarian formulation.

The other Italian doctor was Stancaro, whom Isabella highly commended when he made a trip to Poland. This did not mean an endorsement of his views which at that time had not yet been formulated. He began to be perplexed to see how Christ as God could act as a mediator between man and God, and arrived at the conclusion that he had done so only in his human nature. Was then the human nature placating the divine nature? The simplest solution was to deny that Christ was God. This step was taken by the Hungarian Dévai, who abandoned the worship of Christ. These deviators from orthodoxy had the support of Sigismund Zapolya. The son of Isabella was the only Unitarian king in history.

## BIBLIOGRAPHY

*Bibliography:*
   *Guide to Hungarian Studies,* vol. 1 (Stanford, Cal., 1973).

*General Histories of Transylvania:*
   Bethlen, Wolffgangi de, *Historia de Rebus Transylvaniis,* 2d. ed. Tome 1 (1782).
   Forgacs, Ferenz, *Rerum Hungaricarium—Commentarii,* (1788).
   Makkai, Ladislas, *Histoire de Transylvanie* (Paris, 1946).

*The Religious Situation:*

Bucsay, Mihály, *Geschichte des Protestantismus in Ungarn* (Stuttgart, 1959), compact.

Kalman, Benda, "La Reforme en Hongrie," *Bulletin* de la Société de *l'Histoire du Protestantisme Français* CXXII (1976), pp. 1-53. He explains the varieties of Protestantism and the shifts in the several sections in terms of the economic and social situations.

Lampe, Adolf, *Historia Ecclesiae Reformatae in Hungaria et Transylvania* (1728).

Pirnat, Antal, "Die Ideologie der Siebenbürger Antitrinitarier in den 1570en Jahren," *Ungarische Akademie der Wissenschaften* (1961).

Roth, Erick, *Die Reformation in Siebenbürgen* (1962).

St. Ivanyi, (In Hungarian St. stands for Szent), Alexander, *Freedom Legislation in Hungary, 1557-1571* (New York, 1957).

Teutsch, Friedrich, *Geschichte der ev. Kirche in Siebenbürgen*, vol. 1 (1921).

Wilbur, E. Morse, *A History of Unitarianism*, vol. II (Cambridge, Mass.) (1952).

Williams, George H., *The Radical Reformation* (Philadelphia, 1962).

Wittstock, Oskar, *Johannes Honterus* (Göttingen, 1970).

*Isabella:*

Veress, Endre, (Veress is the family name) *Izabella Királyné* (Budapest, 1901). (Borrowed from the Harvard Library.) The work is in Hungarian which I do not read. There is an epitome of the work by A. Veress, *Isabella regina d'Ungheria* (Rome, 1903), of which my friend Prof. Lamberti Borghi has sent me a xerox. From the Hungarian I have taken several illustrations. The tracts entitled *Vier warhafftige Missiven* (1542), contain one by her and the rest about her. Copy in the Beinecke Library of Yale University.

*The Turks:*

Hammer, T.de, *Histoire de l'Empire Ottoman* (Paris, 1896), translated from German.

Merriman, Roger Bigelow, *Suleiman the Magnificant 1520-1566* (Cambridge, Mass., 1944).

Savage, J., *The Turkish History* (1704).

Wagner, Georg, *Das Türkenjahr 1664* (Eisenstadt, 1964).

Wrancius, Antonius, *Expeditionis Solymani in Moldavium et Transylcanium Libri Duo* (Budapest, 1944).

The Beinecke Library has five boxes of tracts on the Turkish threat in the sixteenth century. They are itemized in the shelf list.

## NOTES

1. Forgacs, p. 208, Bethlen, p. 288, Makkai, p. 134.
2. Bethlen, p. 275.
3. Bethlen, pp. 334-47.
4. Bethlen, pp. 350-52.
5. *Vier warhrafftige.* See bibliography and illustration.
6. Opinion differs as to whether Martinuzzi was a statesman or a scamp. Makkai regards him as the former and his reason seems plausible.
7. Huber.
8. St. Ivanyi. Latin text in the appendix.

# Helena Mezeo

The women chosen to represent Hungary and Transylvania were not natives. Maria was Spanish and German. Isabella was Polish and Italian. A Hungarian friend has given me the names of several native women influential in the reform. Unhappily the books, even if accessible in this country, are in Hungarian, which to my chagrin I cannot read. I could, of course, enlist friends to translate, but luckily the account of one woman is in Latin, and for that reason she is my choice. Her distinction lies in what she did on behalf of Stephen Szegedi, one of the most outstanding Hungarian reformers. He was well versed in Renaissance scholarship as well as in Catholic and Protestant theology. While a Catholic he studied at Vienna. Later he was three years at the University of Wittenberg under the tutelage of Luther and Melanchthon. Szegedi's spiritual pilgrimage passed through Catholicism, Lutheranism, Zwinglianism, to Calvinism. He did not take the further road to Unitarianism.

In the early years of his evangelizing in Hungarian territory he suffered imprisonment and banishment but invariably re-entered the field. Ordinarily he combined preaching and teaching. Severe trouble overtook him in 1562 because the town in which he was located was dilatory in paying tribute to the Turk. The voivode reported the delinquency to his superior, Mamhut Begus, who sent in Turkish troops and arrested two of the leading citizens as hostages, of whom one was Szegedi. He was very

Stephen Szegedi

much more of a leading citizen than the Turk ever suspected. As a teacher and preacher he was held in high esteem by all the populace and the notables, doubly so because his tone toward the Catholics was irenic.

Protest from all classes came to the ear of Begus, who inferred that Szegedi was of such prominence that he could be held for a superlative ransom. The sum of a thousand florins was suggested.

The economic reason for detention was strengthened by the suspicion that, in evangelizing beyond his bailiwick, Szegedi was actually engaged in political machinations. In all of this running around what was he up to? Torture was used to find out. He was kept in the vilest squalor and suspended till scarcely alive. A visitor saw his shirt blood soaked. Visitors were permitted, perhaps because the money they left for him was confiscated.

Turks taking Christians captive

His supporters suggested that he be exchanged for a prisoner held by the Hungarians, the daughter of a high Turkish official. Begus replied that he could not be sure they would deliver the right girl. An ardent Muslim came to convert Szegedi, and, if I correctly understand the passage, the suggestion was made that release might be granted if he were to translate the Koran into Hungarian.

Now we come to Helena, the wife of Firenc Mezeo, a peasant farmer. She suggested to her husband that he go to Vienna and try to persuade the Turkish emissary there resident to use his influence for the release. He proved to be like Pilate, who desired to release Jesus and like Claudius Lysias, who would have liberated Paul. The Turk would try.

Now Helena, following childbirth, was smitten by a lethal disease. Dying, she laid it upon her husband to exert every nerve to free Szegedi. In tears he swore. But when his concern was laid before a church assembly he was told to wait until the Lord opened a more seasonable opportunity. Word of the renewed clamor reached the ear of Begus, perhaps through the Pontius Pilate in Vienna. When the Begus became aware that the instigator of the fresh agitation was a mere peasant, all suspicion of espionage was at once dispelled. "A peasant!" ejaculated Begus. "Then he can be trusted." But the Turk was of no mind to renounce the ransom which was eventually raised to 1200 florins. Then he who had sworn to a dying wife raised the sum. From France and Germany breastplates, helmets and corselets were imported for payment in kind. "Thus," records the chronicler, "this peasant, moved by the immeasurable liberality of Christ, was able to achieve the goal." A mighty concourse greeted the return, having prearranged that Szegedi should be a witness at the wedding of his eldest daughter.

## BIBLIOGRAPHY

Summarized from *Stephani Szegedini Vita Avctore Matthaeo Scaricaeo Pannonio*, which is prefaced to the *Theologiae Sincerae Loci Communes* (Basel, 1599). In the Beinecke Library of Yale University.

# Illustrations

138    Sigismund I from Marcin Kromer, *De Origine et rebus gestis Polonorum* (Basel, 1555), p. 184. Beinecke Rare Book and Manuscript library, Yale University.

142    Miniature from the Prayer Book of Queen Bona with permission from the Bodleian Library.

144    Budny's translation of the Bible into Polish from Henryk Biegeleisen, *Illustrowane dzieje literatury polskiej* (Wieden, 1898) III, p. 184.

147    Sigismund Augustus, same source as for Sigismund I.

148    Barbara Radziwill. Michał Balinsky, *Pisma Historyczne* (Warsaw, 1843), borrowed from the University of Washington library.

152    Queen Bona widowed, from Eugeniusz Gołebiowski, *Zygmunt August* (Warsaw, 1962). The author says that the painting was done in 1530, but the medal calls her a widow which she became in 1548.

161    The Crab on the device of Gnoinskiej from Franciszek, Piekesinski, *Heraldyka Polska* (Kraków, 1899), p. 171.

166    From Stanisław Cynarskiego ed. *Rakow Ognisko Arianizmu* (Kraków, 1968), p. 176, redrawn with omission of some details.

170    Zofia Olneska, Biegeleisen, *Opus. cit.*, p. 222, pl. 88.

171    Home teaching in prayer, from Biegeleisen, *opus cit.*, p. 220. Hymn singing in the home, from Lissa Zofia, *Muzyka polsiego Odrocizenia* (Warsaw, 1953).

172    Musical setting from K.WT. Koicicki, *Biblioteka Starozytnych polskich*, I Wyd. (Kraków, 1854), pp. 9 ff. Harvard Library.

182    Katarina Jagellonica. Courtesy of the National Museum, Nürnberg.

190    "Communion in Both Kinds in 1548." From the *Handbook*. From Hjalmar Holmquist, Svenska Kyrkans Historia. Pt. I, p. 427. Svenska Kyrkans Diakonistyrelses Bokforlag, Stockholm. 1933.

193    "The Augsburg Confession in Swedish in 1566 with the Swedish coat of arms and a dedication to King John's sister, the Princess Elizabeth." *Ibid.*, Pt. II, p. 109.

202    Portions of the Funeral Procession of John III Clergy to the left. From Emil Hildebrand, *Sveriges Historia V*, pp. 236-7. P. A. Nostedt & Somers Forlag, Stockholm, 1923.

206    Maria of Hungary. Courtesy Szepmuveszeti Müseum, Budapest. Description in A. Pilger, *Katalog der Galerie alter Meister* (Budapest, 1967), p. 434.

207    Maria and Louis II of Hungary from Georg Hirth, *Bilder aus der Lutherzeit* (München, 1883), pl. 485-6.

# *Index*